CHRISTIAN SECTS IN THE NINETEENTH CENTURY IN A SERIES OF LETTERS TO A LADY

Caroline Frances Cornwallis

"By this shall all men know that ye are my disciples if ye have love one to another."

—John xiii. 35.

"Heaven and Hell are not more distant, than the benevolent spirit of the Gospel, and the malignant spirit of party. The most impious wars ever made were called

—'Holy Wars.'"Lyttleton.

"Let those ill-invented terms whereby we have been distinguished from each other be swallowed up in that name which will lead us hand in hand to heaven

—the name of Christian." Bishop Ryder.

The following letters grew out of a conversation between one of the editors of the "Small Books," and a lady of his acquaintance; and as there are probably many who have felt the want of the information they contain, it has been thought that by publishing them in a collected form they may be useful. The views of the writer are sufficiently explained in the letters themselves. All lament the small sum of Christian charity to be found among religionists in general, but few when they begin to write have kept clear of a severity of comment which but prolongs differences. The writer, himself a member of the Church of England, is anxious to show that it is possible to be attached to one persuasion without imputing either folly or ill intention to others; and it is with a view of promoting the loving fellowship of all whom God disdains not to create and support, that this slight sketch is given to the world.

LETTER I.

You some time ago requested me to give you the result of my inquiries into the tenets of the different religious sects which I had been acquainted with; and respecting which we had at different times conversed. In the time which has since elapsed I have been endeavouring, both to ascertain them more completely, and to compare them with what I conceive to be the true spirit of Christianity; but the subject has so grown as I proceeded, that even now I can only give you a very short, and I fear, in some cases, an imperfect notion of them. Yet the subject is one of deep interest; and as I feel convinced that if we looked a little closer into the differences between the established church and those who separate from it, both parties would find them smaller and less important than they imagine, and that Christian charity would be increased by the examination, I do not shrink from the task however inadequately I may execute it.

I propose therefore to show you by extracts from the works of the principal writers among the different religious sects, how they all agree in most of the fundamental doctrines of Christianity; at the same time that I point out the evil consequences which I conceive would ensue were some of their tenets *fully carried out* into practice: and also to state wherein their peculiar opinions appear to me to be opposed to "the truth as it is in Christ Jesus," so far as to prevent me from adopting them; though I can fully believe that those who hold these opinions in the abstract, may, notwithstanding, be excellent practical Christians.

Firmly attached as I am to the Church of England, whose form of worship (allowing for the imperfections which naturally cling to all human institutions), I consider preferable to any other; I can still see much to admire in other persuasions and other ceremonies, mixed up, though it be, with some imperfections and error; and my love to the established church does not blind me to some matters which might be better otherwise, and which I shall point out as I proceed.

"Of all the Christian graces," says a quaint writer, "zeal is the most apt to turn sour;" and the observation is no less true than it is sad, for men too seldom remember that they must add to their faith knowledge, and that both are of no avail without the crowning gift of charity,[1] or in other words, brotherly love for all mankind. The real Christian, it seems to me, should imitate the liberality of St. Paul, who, after having been bred up in the habits of the "strictest sect" of the Jews, scrupled not to quit all his former prejudices, in order to preach Christ to the Gentiles, without disgusting them by ceremonies which were no fundamental part of the religion he taught, and was content to become "as a Jew, that he might gain the Jews, and to them that were without law, to become as without law (being not without law to God), that he might by all means save some."[2]

We are too apt to hold each other accountable for all the consequences which can be logically deduced from an opinion, however extreme they may be: and then having persuaded ourselves that those abstract tenets which, by straining them to an extreme point, *may* have an evil effect, *must* have an evil effect on all who profess them,—we avoid those who differ from us on religious subjects, because we have assumed that they are actually immoral by virtue of their opinions; and thus we miss the opportunity of convincing ourselves of our mistake by a more intimate knowledge of their lives. "By their fruits ye shall know them," says our Lord; but we seldom approach them closely enough to see the fruits.

---

[1] αγαπη which is the word generally translated *charity* in the New Testament means *affectionate regard*. The distinction between charity and almsgiving is well laid down by St. Clement of Alexandria. "Charity," says he, "leads to the sharing our good things with others; but this is not in itself charity, but only our outward sign of that feeling."

[2] See I Cor. ix. 19, 20.

If we would be content to sink minor differences, and be satisfied that "in every nation he that feareth God and worketh righteousness is accepted with him," we should soon meet on better terms; for we do not hold at a distance from those on earth whom we expect to meet in heaven; and thanks be to God, there is no religious persuasion that cannot boast of many such as Cornelius.

St. Paul recommends to the churches that they be "kindly affectioned one towards another, in honour preferring one another:"[3] "by this shall men know that ye are my disciples," says our Great Exemplar, "if ye have love one to another;" but alas! if we contemplate what is called the Christian world, where shall we find Christ's *true* disciples? Grievous indeed it is, as has been well observed, that that religion, which "should most correct and sweeten men's spirits, sours and sharpens them the most." But surely "*we* have not so learned Christ." Let us for a moment contemplate His conduct towards those who differed from him in religious opinions; his compassion towards them; his meek reproofs not only to the Sadducees and the Samaritans, but even to the more hardened;[4] and then let us turn to our own hearts and confess with shame that we have fallen miserably short of that charity without which "whosoever liveth is counted dead before God."

---

[3] Rom. xii. 10.

[4] "No national prejudices, no religious differences could hinder our Saviour from doing good. We should consider that men's understandings naturally are not all of the same size and capacity, and that this difference is greatly increased by different education, different employments, different company, and the like. No man is infallible. We are liable to errors perhaps as much as others. The very best men may sometimes differ in opinion, as St. Paul 'withstood St. Peter to the face;' and if there was such a difference between two of the chiefest of the Apostles, well may there be between inferior mortals. About modes of faith there will always be dispute and difference; but in acts of mercy and kindness all mankind may and should agree."—*Newton.*

So clear is the command to exercise universal benevolence, that whatever obscurity there may be in other parts of Scripture, however men, even wise ones, may differ as to the real signification of certain passages in the Bible, *here* at least there can be no cavilling. It is intelligible to the most ignorant as well as the most learned, so that "the wayfaring man, though a fool, shall not err therein."

Archbishop Tillotson relates of Mr. Gouge, an eminent nonconformist, that he allowed men to differ from him in opinions that were "*very dear* to him;" and provided men did but "fear God and work righteousness," he loved them heartily, how distant soever from him in judgment about things less necessary: "in all which," observes the Archbishop, "he is very worthy to be a pattern to men of all persuasions." "I abhor two principles in religion," says William Penn in a letter to the same archbishop, "and pity them that own them. The first is obedience upon authority without conviction; and the other, destroying them that differ from me for God's sake: such a religion is without judgment, though not without truth. Union is best, if right; if not, charity."

I have given the opinion of these two eminent men of different persuasions, partly to show that the evil I complain of is one of long standing; partly to justify my own opinion as to the remedy; namely, the paying *more* attention to the fundamental doctrines of Christianity; *less*, to those minor differences which, from the very obscurity of the texts on which they are founded, come more frequently under discussion, and thus, from a mental operation somewhat analogous to that of the laws of perspective, seem large and important because they are close under our eyes, though they are in fact minute in comparison with those which we have not been examining so closely. Thus men inadvertently reverse the order of things, and zeal for the maintenance of peculiar tenets too often supersedes the far more important virtue of Christian benevolence, to the scandal of all good Christians and the mockery of unbelievers.

The Quakers, in their address to James II. on his accession, told him that they understood he was no more of the established religion than themselves. "We therefore hope," said they, "that thou wilt allow us that liberty which thou takest thyself:" and it would be well if we took a hint from this, and reflected that we differ as much from other sects as they do from us,[5] and that the greatest heresy is, as a Christian Father declared it to be long ago—"a wicked life."

It is, however, needful to distinguish between the Christian spirit of forbearance towards those who differ from us in religious opinions, which Christ and his apostles so strongly inculcate, and the indolent latitudinarianism which induces many to declare that "a man cannot help his belief," that "sincerity is everything," that "all religious sects are alike," &c.: positions which, as you well observed on one occasion, ought rather to be reversed; for when men are *not* sincere, all sects certainly *are* alike: for then it is but a lip service which will never influence the life, and it matters not what opinion is professed; it will be equally powerless.

---

[5] "In fact, all the religious persecutions in the world, all the penalties and inflictions upon those who differ from ourselves, however conscientiously, take their rise from an imperfect and erroneous notion of what really constitutes the glory of God, and the manner in which we best can assist its display and extension. The angels at the birth of Christ sang that the glory of God was in unison with 'Peace on earth, and good will towards men.'—'No!' said the Schoolman, 'the glory of God consists in thinking of the Deity as we think.'—'No!' said the Inquisitor, 'the glory of God consists in worshiping as we prescribe.'—'No!' said the Covenanters, 'the glory of God consists in exterminating those whom we call his enemies.' Mistaken men! who *thus* propose to honour the God and Father of the universe, the merciful God, and the gracious Father of all his rational creatures! Instead of perusing with delight and conviction the plain declaration contained in our Sacred records, too many Christians have in almost every age passed over the characteristics of kind design throughout nature: they have mistaken or forgotten the clear delineations of Divine Mercy and Goodness in the Book of Grace, and have had recourse to the narrowed circle of their own prejudices."—*Maltby's Sermons.*

Sincere belief must be the consequence of proof, without which we cannot believe truly; with it, we must. If then we content ourselves with the mere *ipse dixit* of others without seeking proof, our belief is the result of indolence, and for that indolence we shall be accountable when we are called on to give an account of the talent committed to our charge, if error has been consequent upon it. He, on the contrary, whose education or whose means have not put proof within his reach, although he may wish earnestly for it, *may* be wrong in understanding, but he will never be wrong in heart: his tenets may be wrong, but his life will be right. It behoves us therefore to be cautious how we pass sentence on one another in religious matters, since, as has been well observed, we are ourselves amenable to a tribunal where uncharitable conduct towards others, will bring down a just and heavy sentence on ourselves. We are not to erect ourselves into judges of other men's consciences,[6] but leave them to the judgment and disposal of One who alone can see into the heart of men, and alone can ascertain the real nature and ultimate consequence of all questions which admit of "doubtful disputation."

There will be some danger of losing our way among the almost numberless divisions and subdivisions of sects, which present themselves as soon as we begin to consider the subject at all narrowly. I therefore propose to simplify my task, and make our course a little plainer, by adopting the two great divisions into which the reformed churches may have been said to have arranged themselves at the era of the Reformation, as a foundation for the classification of Christian sects at present. Calvin and Melancthon may be considered as the prototypes and heads of these two divisions, which however they may sometimes vary and sometimes intermingle, are continually reproduced, because they are grounded upon two great natural divisions of human kind, the stern and the gentle. My own leaning is to the latter, because it appears to me most in accordance with the spirit of that gospel

---

[6] It would be well if Rom. xiv. were more attentively studied and more universally practised among Christians.

whose great Promulgator made universal benevolence the test of his disciples; but at the same time I must acknowledge, and shall indeed prove before I have done, that the sterner theoretical view may coexist in the mind with a large share of true Christian charity and benevolence. Be the abstract belief of the Christian what it may, if he be really at heart a disciple, the example of his mild Master will always influence his life and feelings, and he will tread in the steps of his Lord, even if his judgment should sometimes have mistaken the true meaning of some of his words.

These two views of the Divine dispensations towards man were first arrayed in actual hostility at the Synod of Dort in 1618, where the doctrines of James Arminius, professor of divinity in the University of Leyden, who had followed the opinions of Luther and Melancthon, were condemned, and those of the Calvinistic church of Geneva affirmed. From that time the various sects of the reformed church have generally been known as Arminian or Calvinistic, according as they embraced the peculiar tenets of either party on the subject of man's salvation: I shall therefore thus distinguish the two classes into which I propose to arrange them, though they may not follow out either in the whole of their opinions.

I. Arminian.

1. Quakers.

2. Socinians and Unitarians.

3. Wesleyan Methodists.

4. General Baptists, Moravians, Swedenborgians, Plymouth Brethren.

II. Calvinistic.

1. Presbyterians, Independents.

2. Particular Baptists, Sub and Supralapsarians, Sandemanians.

3. Calvinistic Methodists. Evangelical or Low Church.

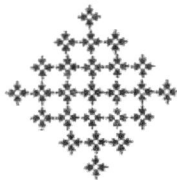

LETTER II.

QUAKERS.

The sect which I have placed first upon my list, arose about the middle of the seventeenth century, when a number of individuals withdrew from the communion of every *visible* church "to seek,"[7] as they expressed it, "the Lord, in retirement:" and George Fox, their leader, or as they termed him, their "honourable elder," went about preaching their opinions in fairs and markets, in courts of justice, and steeple houses, i.e. churches. He denounced the state worship as "superstitious," and warned all to obey the Holy Spirit, speaking by him. He was in consequence brought before two justices of the peace in Derbyshire in 1650, one of whom, Mr. Bennet, called Fox, and his hearers "Quakers," in derision of their frequent admonitions to "*tremble* at the Word of God;" and this appellation soon became general, though they themselves took then, and still preserve, the title of "the Society of Friends."

The rigid peculiarities of phrase, &c. which Fox added to his religious sentiments; the regular discipline which he enforced; and the zeal with which he maintained and propagated his tenets gave consistency to this sect, although he was not, as has been supposed, the originator of their doctrines. He conceived himself forbidden by divine command to pull off his hat to any one, or to address any one excepting in the singular number, or to "call any man master;" and for these peculiarities as well as for the refusal to give or accept titles of honour, or to take an oath, the "Friends" suffered the most cruel persecutions; for we are told that "they tortured with cruel whippings the bodies of both men

---

[7] They have in consequence been sometimes called "Seekers."

and women of good estate and reputation;"[8] and were further punished by impounding of their horses; by distress of goods; by fines, imprisonments, whipping, and setting in the stocks:[9] yet, notwithstanding these severities, the sect increased and spread far and wide, and great numbers of people were drawn together, many out of animosity, to hear them.

The Declaration of Indulgence in 1663 stopped for a short time the persecution of the Quakers, but by the Conventicle Act of 1664, numbers of them were condemned to transportation: in 1666, however, their condition improved, when the celebrated William Penn, the son of Admiral Penn, joined them.

The discipline of this society is kept up by monthly meetings, composed of an aggregate of several particular congregations, whose business it is to provide for the maintenance of their poor, and the education of their children; also to judge of the sincerity and fitness of persons desirous of being admitted as members; to direct proper attention to religion and moral duty; and to deal with disorderly members. At each monthly meeting persons are appointed to see that the rules of their discipline are put in practice. It is usual when any member has misconducted himself, to appoint a small committee to visit the offender, to endeavour to convince him of his error and induce him to forsake it. If they succeed, he is declared to have "made satisfaction for his offence," otherwise he is dismissed from the society. In disputes between individuals, it is enjoined that the members of this sect should not sue each other at law, but settle their differences by the rules of the society.

Marriage is regarded by the Quakers as a religious, not a mere civil compact. Those who wish to enter into that state appear together, and state their intentions at one of the monthly meetings, and if not attended by parents or guardians must produce their consent in writing duly witnessed; and if no objections are raised at a subsequent meeting, they are allowed to

---

[8] Gough's History of the Quakers. Vol. i. p. 139.
[9] Probably their resolute refusal to pay tithes and other dues brought on them some of these punishments.

solemnize their marriage, which is done at a public meeting for worship; towards the close of which the parties stand up and solemnly take each other for man and wife. A certificate of the proceedings is then read publicly and signed by the parties, and afterwards by the relations as witnesses. The monthly meeting keeps a register of the marriages as well as of the births and burials of the society.

Children are named without any attending ceremony; neither is it held *needful* that there should be any at burial, though the body followed by the relatives and friends is sometimes carried into a meeting house, and at the grave a pause is generally made to allow of a discourse from any friend attending if he be so inclined.

The women have monthly, quarterly, and yearly meetings of their own sex, but without the power of making rules. "As we believe," they say, "that women may be rightly called to the work of the ministry, we also think that to them belongs a share in the support of Christian discipline; and that some parts of it wherein their own sex is concerned devolve on them with peculiar propriety."

But what, you will ask, are the religious tenets of this sect? The question will perhaps best be answered by an extract from their "Rules of Discipline," a work published under the sanction of the society. "The original and immediate ground of the religious fellowship of the early Friends," says the writer of this manual, "was *union of sentiment in regard to Christ's inward teaching.*" They were firm believers in all that is revealed in Holy Scripture respecting our Lord and Saviour Jesus Christ; nor would they have allowed that any one held the truth who denied his coming in the flesh, or the benefit to fallen man by his propitiatory sacrifice. "We believe that, in order to enable mankind to put in practice the precepts of the gospel, every man coming into the world is endued with a measure of the light, grace, or good Spirit of Christ, by which, as it is alluded to, he is enabled to distinguish good from evil, and to correct the disorderly passions and corrupt propensities of his fallen nature, which *mere reason* is altogether insufficient to overcome. For all that belongs to man is fallible, and within the reach of temptation: but the divine grace, which comes by Him, i.e. Christ, who hath overcome the world, is, to those who humbly and sincerely seek it, an all-sufficient and present help in time of need . . . whereby the soul is translated out of the kingdom of darkness, and from under the power of Satan into the marvellous light and kingdom of the Son of God. Now as we thus believe that the grace of God, which comes by Jesus Christ, is alone sufficient for salvation, we can neither admit that it is conferred upon a few only, while others are left without it; nor thus asserting its universality, can we limit its operation to a partial cleansing of the soul from sin even in this life."

Baptism and the Lord's supper are regarded by this sect as mere types or shadows, representing in a figurative manner certain great particulars of Christian Truths, but not intended to be of permanent obligation. They consider the former to have been superseded by the baptism of the Spirit: of the latter they say, "the emblem may be either used or disused as Christians may consider most conducive to the real advantage of the church: the only *needful* supper of the Lord is altogether of a spiritual nature." They conceive that a reliance on the eucharist as a 'viaticum or saving ordinance,' is a dangerous tenet, as well as the connecting the rite of baptism with regeneration. They think that "ordinances so liable to abuse, and the cause of so many divisions and persecutions, cannot truly appertain to the law of God."

Quakers consider all holidays as "shadows" which ceased with the shadowy dispensations of the law, and that neither the first day of the week, nor any other, possesses any superior sanctity; [10]but as a society they have never objected to "a day of

---

[10] "Keep the Sabbath holy," says Luther, "for its use both to body and soul; but if any where the day is made holy for the mere day's sake; if any where any one sets up its observance upon a *Jewish* foundation, then I order you to work on it, to ride on it, to dance on it, to feast on it, to do any thing that shall remove this encroachment on the Christian spirit and liberty." This is language which may be easily misunderstood

rest," for the purpose of religious improvement. They consider the Christian Dispensation to have superseded the use of oaths, and contend that our Lord's precepts[11] extend even to the swearing of witnesses in courts of law. War they hold to be altogether inconsistent with the spirit and precepts of the gospel, and urge that the primitive Christians during two centuries maintained its unlawfulness. They object on the same principle to capital punishments, and the slave trade.

The members of the society are bound by their principles to abstain entirely "from profane and extravagant entertainments," from excess in eating and drinking; from public diversions; from the reading of useless, frivolous, and pernicious books; from gaming of every description; and from vain and injurious sports (such as hunting or shooting for diversion); from unnecessary display in funerals, furniture, and style of living: from unprofitable, seductive, and dangerous amusements, among which are ranked dancing and music; and generally from all "such occupations of time and mind as plainly tend to levity, vanity, and forgetfulness of our God and Saviour," and they object to all complimentary intercourse.

In the sketch I have now given of the tenets of this sect, you cannot have failed to observe how closely their notions with regard to the fundamental doctrines of Christianity tally with those of the great body of the church; the differences being all on points of minor import, if we except the ceremonies of baptism and the Lord's supper; which, being the appointment of Christ himself, we are not at liberty to reject. And yet, be it observed, the Quaker does not presumptuously reject them, but merely acts upon, as we suppose, an erroneous view of their nature.

On points of minor difference it may be observed, that He who was the Prince of Peace, and came to establish it, never specifically forbad war, (for there may be cases where it is merely self defence,) but left it to the spirit of the gospel to remove the

---

and perverted from Luther's meaning; but it was uttered by him from a jealousy of Sabbatical superstition.

[11] Matt. v.

causes of war.[12] We all know the appellation bestowed on the Centurion, Cornelius: and when soldiers came to John the Baptist saying, "What shall we do?" he merely sought to retrench the disorders and injustice which those who follow the profession of arms might be tempted to commit; but did not condemn their necessary employments. We may therefore fairly conclude that the sweeping condemnation of *all* war by the Quakers, is not warranted by Scripture, although it is in many and indeed most instances, entered upon far too carelessly.

One of the main distinctions of the Quakers is the rejection of certain amusements and pursuits, which others on the contrary consider as innocent, believing that the religion of Christ rather encourages than forbids a cheerful spirit, and allows by the example of the Saviour, a participation in social pleasures: and that "an upright, religious man, by partaking in such pleasures, may be the means of restraining others within due bounds, and by his very presence may prevent their degenerating into extravagance, profligacy, and sin;"[13] and such do not feel in their

---

[12] "There is an unreasonable, uncharitable, and superstitious notion that a soldier, so far as his profession is concerned, is 'of the world;' and that a man who dies in the field of battle is *necessarily* less prepared for his change than one who dies in his bed. These feelings, which have sadly tended to degrade and impoverish the mind of modern Europe . . . to make armies what they are told they *must* be; and therefore to make them dangerous by depriving them of any high restraining principles, have been greatly encouraged by the tone which religious men of our day have adopted from the Quakers." *Maurice's Kingdom of Christ.*

[13] Moral education, in spite of all the labours of direct instruction, is really acquired in hours of recreation. Sports and amusements are, and must be the means by which the mind is insensibly trained: 'Men are but children of a larger growth;' they will have their pleasures; and unless care be taken, the sermon of the church or chapel will be neutralized by the association of the tavern and the raceground. There must be safety valves for the mind, i.e. there must be means for its pleasurable, profitable, and healthful exertion; those means it is in our power to render safe and innocent; in too many instances they have been rendered dangerous and guilty." *Dr. Taylor.*

hearts that *these*[14] are the "pomps and vanities of the world," which by their baptismal vow they renounce. But surely it is possible that different persons may regard the same pursuits and amusements in a very different light, and yet both may be conscientious in their views, and both, whether in abstaining or enjoying, be equally doing that which is lawful and right in the sight of God. That very amusement or pursuit which is a snare to one, and therefore to be avoided by him, may be a source of innocent, and perhaps profitable recreation to another. It is the intention, the *animus* with which an act is done, and not the act itself which constitutes the sin. "Let not him that eateth despise him that eateth not; and let not him that eateth not judge him that eateth: to his own master he standeth or falleth."

"Christianity," says an excellent prelate of our church, "forbids no necessary occupation, no reasonable indulgences, no innocent relaxation. It allows us to 'use' the world, provided we do not 'abuse' it. It does not spread before us a delicious banquet, and then come with a 'Touch not, taste not, handle not:' all it requires is that our liberty degenerate not into licentiousness; our amusements into dissipation; our industry into incessant toil; our carefulness into extreme anxiety and endless solicitude. When it requires us to be 'temperate in all things,' it plainly tells us that we *may* use all things temperately.[15] When it directs us to

---

[14] Every creature of God is good, and nothing to be refused if it be received with thanksgiving. (I Tim. iv. 4.) Extend this maxim, apply it to the several means of enjoyment, either supposed or real, that the world presents to us. Those pleasures from which we cannot unreservedly arise, and thank our Maker; those pursuits which mar our devotions, and render us unwilling or afraid to come before Him, cannot be innocent. It would be no easy matter to lay down, as applicable to all, a rule as to how far conformity with the world is admissible, and where the Christian must stop: for as the habits and tempers and propensities of men differ, so also do their temptations and their danger. Thus through the rule by which one would stand securely, another would as certainly fall. *Lectures on the Church Catechism.*

[15] See I Tim. iv. 4.

'make our moderation known unto all men,' this evidently implies that within the bounds of moderation we may enjoy all the reasonable conveniences and comforts of this present life."

I have noticed this, in my opinion, erroneous practice of the Quakers at the more length, because it is not confined to them. Asceticism, of which this is one branch, has been the bane of the church and of Christianity generally; and few sects are entirely free from the notion that holiness requires a withdrawal from amusements, and a certain degree of seclusion from the world. Yet, if the world is to be improved, the leaven must be placed *in* it; and a good man probably never does his Father's work more effectually than when he spreads the sanctifying influence of his example through all the relations of life; showing that there is no position in society where Christianity does not add a grace and a relish unknown without it: spreading refinement of manners and delicacy of thought, and insensibly rendering social intercourse more polished, and more delightful, by banishing from it all that can offend.

The Quakers adduce Matt. v. 33–37, James v. 12, &c. in support of their objection to all oaths, even judicial ones, and consider that the Christian dispensation abrogated their use. But in answer to this we may observe that even the Almighty is represented as confirming his promises by a solemn oath. "Because," says the apostle, "He could swear by no higher, He sware by Himself;" and St. Paul on particular occasions expresses himself thus, "As God is true:" "Before God I lie not:" "God is my record," &c. all which expressions undoubtedly contain the essence and formality of an oath; and the Apostle upon some occasions mentions this solemn swearing with approbation, "an oath for confirmation is the end of all strife:" the swearing, therefore, which our Saviour absolutely forbids, is common or unnecessary swearing, and we are recommended to affirm or deny in common conversation without imprecations. "Let your conversation be yea, yea,—nay, nay."

The repugnance entertained by the Quakers against paying tithes appears to me to arise from an error in their mode of viewing the question. The assertion made by them "that all the provision made for ministers of the gospel in the first ages was made by the love of their flocks," is true, though that love very soon produced endowments, even before Christianity was established as the law of the empire. But allowing this, it does not follow, as they go on to assert, that "since we are under the same dispensation of love as the Apostles were, the principles which governed the church then are to govern it now." Tithes were originally given to the church as a corporation, by the owners of the soil; and since that time estates have been transferred from hand to hand subject to that charge, till no man has any plea for refusing it. The question is not one of religion but of property. If my estate devolve to me chargeable with an annuity payable either to a corporation or an individual, I have no right to set up his religious opinions in bar of his claim: for I have paid less for the purchase in consequence of the existence of that claim, which in common honesty therefore I am bound to satisfy, be the annuitant who he may. [16]

Having now noticed the points wherein I consider the peculiar tenets of the Quakers to be erroneous, I shall conclude with the more agreeable part of my task, and prove by extracts from one of their writers how much of true Christian feeling exists among them. The following is from a little book given me by a Quaker, from the pen of J. Gurney, entitled "An Essay on Love to God."

---

[16] "A reverend Doctor in Cambridge was troubled at his small living at Hoggenton (Oakington) with a peremptory Anabaptist, who plainly told him, 'It goes against my conscience to pay you tithes except you can show me a place of Scripture whereby they are due unto you.' The Dr. returned, 'Why should it not go as much against my conscience that you should enjoy your nine parts for which you can show no place in Scripture?' To whom the other rejoined, 'But I have for my land deeds and evidences from my fathers, who purchased and were peaceably possessed thereof by the laws of the land.' 'The same is my title,' said the Doctor, 'tithes being confirmed unto me by many statutes of the land, time out of mind.'" *Fuller's Church History, Book II.*

"Still more completely than the provisions of nature fall in with our bodily state, and supply our temporal wants; still more properly than the air agrees with the functions of the lungs, and the light with those of the eye, does the gospel of our Redeemer suit the spiritual condition of man. We are a fallen race, alienated from God by our sins, justly liable to his wrath: in the gospel we have pardon, peace and restoration. 'Christ made all things new,' says Grotius, 'and the latter creation is *more divine* than the former.' If then the first creation of mankind and all the bounties of nature are the result of Love, that attribute is far more gloriously displayed in the scheme of redemption and in the works of grace.—The love of God the Father is ever represented in Scripture as the origin of all our hopes,—as the eternal, unfathomable spring of the waters of life and salvation, and this love is plainly described as extending to the whole world. 'God so loved the world, &c.[17] God was in Christ reconciling the world to himself'[18]—'God would have all men to be saved, &c.'[19] Do we ask for an overwhelming evidence of the love of God? Let the Apostle satisfy our inquiry. 'In this was manifested the love of God towards us, because God sent his only begotten Son into the world that we might live by him. Herein is love; not that we loved God, but that he loved us, and sent his Son to be the propitiation for our sins.'[20] Do we ask whether God thus loved the whole or only a part of the world?—Let the same Apostle answer: 'He tasted death for *every man*—He gave himself a ransom for *all*, &c.' Even the Gentiles, who were without the benefit of an outward revelation, were by no means destitute of an inward knowledge of the law of God, and some of them showed 'the work of the law written on their hearts, their consciences also bearing witness.'[21] 'Christ is the true light which lighteth every

---

[17] John iii. 16.
[18] 2 Cor. v. 19.
[19] I Tim. ii. 4.
[20] I John iv. 9, 10.
[21] Rom. ii. 15.

man that cometh into the world.'[22] Hence we may reasonably infer that as God appointed the death of Christ to be a sacrifice for the sins of the *whole* world, so *all* men receive through Christ a measure of moral and spiritual light, and all have their day of gracious visitation. If the light in numberless instances be extremely faint, if the darkness fail to comprehend it, we may rest in the conviction that God is not only just but equitable, and that those 'who know not their Master's will and do it not shall be beaten with few stripes.'[23] The gospel of our Lord Jesus Christ, as it is revealed in the Holy Scriptures, is intended for the benefit of the whole world: it is adapted to men of every condition, clime, and character: all are invited to avail themselves of its benefits: all who *will* come *may* come, and 'take the water of life freely.'"

---

[22] John i. 9. See also I John ii. I, 2. 2 Heb. ii. 9.
[23] Luke xii. 48.

LETTER III.

SOCINIANS AND UNITARIANS.

When the first great movement which led to the Reform of a large part of the Christian Churches in Europe, awakened men's minds from the lethargy in which they had slept whilst learning was confined to the cloister, the questions with regard to the nature of the Deity which had distracted the early church began again to be mooted; and as early as the year 1524, "the divinity of Christ was openly denied by Lewis Hetyer, one of the wandering and fanatical Anabaptists, who was put to death at Constance."[24] He was succeeded by Michael Servede or Servetus, a Spanish physician; who, for his wild notions on the same subject, was apprehended on his road through Switzerland at the instigation of Calvin, accused of blasphemy, and condemned to the flames.[25] But doctrines were never yet crushed by persecution, unless indeed it were so wholesale as to exterminate all who held them; and though these opinions were thus fatal to their professors, the main points were reproduced by others; and finally assumed form as a sect, under the titles above named. The term Socinian was taken from two of its most distinguished promoters, Lælius and Faustus Sozinus, or Socinus. They were of an illustrious family at Siena in Tuscany, and Lælius, the uncle of Faustus, having taken a disgust to popery, travelled into France, England, &c. to examine into their religious creed, in order, if possible, to come at the

---

[24] Mosh. Ecc. Hist. Cent. xvi. Sect. iii.
[25] Ib.

truth. He was a man distinguished for his genius and learning, no less than for his virtuous life; he settled at last at Zurich, embraced the Helvetic confession of faith, and died at Zurich in 1562, before he had reached his fortieth year. His sentiments, or rather doubts as to certain points, were embodied, and more openly propagated by his nephew Faustus; who, as is supposed, drew up from his papers the religious system afterwards known under the name of Socinianism. There is however a considerable degree of obscurity hanging over the rise of this sect, and no one has given a satisfactory history of it.

The first appearance of Unitarians, as a distinct congregation, was in Poland, where they obtained a settlement in the city of Cracow in the year 1569; and in 1575 they published at Cracow the "Catechism or Confession of the Unitarians;" [26]but Faustus Socinus having settled among them in the year 1579, soon obtained so much influence as finally to remodel the whole religious system of the sect, and a new form drawn up by Socinus himself, was substituted for the old Catechism.

The following is an abstract of the doctrines taught in this Catechism. After affirming that the Christian religion is "a road for arriving at eternal life, divinely made known," the pupil is told that the will of God on points essential to salvation was revealed by Jesus Christ. The Catechism then goes on to affirm the entire unity of the Deity; since if he is one essence, then must he also be individually one,[27] and therefore Christ cannot he truly said to be a *separate* person or individual, partaking of the *essentia* of the Deity, since that *essentia* is necessarily one. That the Spirit of God, being an essential part of the Deity, cannot be a separate individual (for in this sense the Catechism interprets the word

---

[26] Some of the passages of this Catechism are quoted by Mosheim, which differ very little from the doctrine of the primitive church: all that can be noticed is, that they omit a distinct recognition of the divinity of Christ.

[27] "Fausti Socini Senensis Opera omnia," vol. i. p. 561. These works form a part of the "Bibliotheca Fratrum Polonorum qui Unitarii appellantur." Irenopoli post anno dom. 1656.

persona[28]), any more than his wisdom or his goodness is a separate individual, and that therefore the manifestations of the Spirit of God are manifestations of the Deity himself.

"Christ," says the Catechism, "is a man, according to Rom. v. 15, conceived by a virgin, through the power of the Divine Spirit, without the intervention of man in the ordinary course of generation. He was first subject to suffering and death—afterwards impassible and immortal, Rom. vi. 9. It is in the sense of his existence derived immediately from God, that he, though man, is called the Son of God—as Adam is so termed from the same cause. Jesus Christ was the immediate instrument of God's communications to man; and being, whilst on earth, the voice of God, he is now the anointed King, or Christ, over the people of God."

The passages where he is said to have existed from the beginning: to have created all things, &c. are laboriously explained away, as referring to the regeneration, or new state of things introduced by Christ's mission on earth: and in this part there is much forced interpretation. I shall annex some of the passages in the language of the original,[29] as a proof that I have given a fair account of the real Socinian doctrine, which is very little understood at present. Writers from whom we might expect greater accuracy, have very generally confounded Socinians and Arians, although Faustus Socinus was at the pains to write a laboured refutation of the Arian doctrine, and although a reference to the doctrines of the two sects would show that they are the antipodes of each other. Arius taught that Christ was not of *the same* nature (ὁμοούσιος), with the Father, but of *a like* nature (ὁμοιούσιος) and therefore individually separate—

---

[28] It is remarkable that *persona* should so often be confounded with individual. *Persona* in its original sense was the mask of the actor, *through which the sound* came. The same actor might wear many *personæ*. If Socinus had recollected this, he might have spared himself the trouble of controverting a notion never maintained by the orthodox, i.e. that the Deity was *individually divided.*

[29] Vide Appendix.

separate in will, and capable of differing. This is a direct assertion of two Gods. Socinus on the contrary strenuously asserts the unity of the Deity to the extent of denying the pre-existence of Christ: which Arius though acknowledging that there was a time when he began to exist, nevertheless refers to a period remote beyond human calculation. Thus upon their characteristic doctrines, the two sects are diametrically opposed to each other.

Having now given you the real opinions of Socinus, from his own works, for the book is lying beside me as I write, I shall pursue my plan of examining how far they accord with what was taught by those who certainly ought to be best informed on the subject, namely, Christ himself, his Apostles, and their immediate successors; as well as with the deductions of reason. The unity of the Deity is so frequently and so decidedly asserted in Scripture, that it is impossible to consider any man as unorthodox who professes to make this the groundwork of his belief—so far therefore the Socinian is in accordance both with Scripture and the general voice of the Christian church, for the early Apologists for Christianity, who had to address polytheists, are full of declarations that they worship One only Deity, who by various manifestations has made himself, at different times, known to mankind.[30] There is not a writer of the first and second centuries who does not anxiously assert the one-ness of the God whom the Christians worship: but then they as anxiously assert the identity of their Teacher and Lord with that God. From Christ himself, who says, "Before Abraham was, I am;" [31]"I and the Father are one;"[32] "He who hath seen me hath seen the Father;" "the Father that dwelleth in me, He doeth the works;" [33]to St. Paul, who tells us that "God was in Christ reconciling the world to Himself,"[34] down to the fathers of the early church, to whom I may refer *passim* for the same doctrine; all have distinctly asserted that the

---

[30] Small Books &c. No. VII. p. 21, &c.

[31] πρὶν Ἀβραὰμ γενέσθαι ἐγώ εἰμι.

[32] John. x. 30.

[33] John xiv. 9, 10.

[34] 2 Cor. v. 19.

message of peace to man was delivered by God himself, making use of a human form as the mode of communication with his creatures, and dwelling in "the man Christ Jesus,"[35] as in a temple built up for his especial use; the human nature, to use the expression of the church, "having been taken into God," not the Godhead circumscribed in man. I will not swell the length of my letter with quotations from the fathers which may be found elsewhere; I think the texts I have quoted with many more of the same purport, which you will readily call to mind, suffice to prove that when Socinus asserted the Christ to be *merely* a man, he erred; for though Jesus "the Carpenter's son," as his contemporaries called him, was to all intents and purposes a man "of a reasonable soul and human flesh subsisting;"[36] and though this may be proved from numberless passages in the Scripture, where the man Jesus speaks of his inferiority to the Father and bestower of his human frame and spirit,—yet if we do not entirely distort the meaning of words, *that man* at times uttered declarations of divine power which could only have proceeded from the indwelling Deity, otherwise they must have been the assertions of imposture, which Socinus by no means teaches to have been the case. I know not, therefore, how the believer in the Gospel can avoid acknowledging that Christ was a compound being:— perfectly a man, and speaking as such on some occasions; but, at the same time, the temple of the Ever-living God, whose words flowed from his lips like the answer from the Mercy seat: "Heaven and the heaven of heavens" no doubt "cannot contain" the Infinite; and no true believer will assert that God can be circumscribed in a human body—but, if so mean a comparison may be permitted—as the crater of the volcano is but the mouthpiece of the mighty agents operating within for the fashioning of the earth,—so the manifestation of the Deity in the form, and from the lips of a man, is but that spot of the material creation where the ever blessed Divinity allows himself, as it were, a vent; and gives forth a visible and tangible sign of his existence.

---

[35] I Tim. ii. 5.
[36] Athanasian Creed.

"He that has seen me has seen the Father," says *the Christ.* "I can of my own self do nothing"[37] says *the man:* and this distinction which the Christ who necessarily knew something of the composition of his own nature so frequently asserts, has probably been the groundwork of the mistaken views of this class of Christians, and we may well look with charitable indulgence on the errors of men, who dreading lest they should incur the penalty of giving the incommunicable glory of the Mighty God to another, have not allowed their due weight to the passages, which assert that Mighty God to have undertaken the task of bringing his creature man back to Himself.

Having thus given you a fair account of the creed of Socinus, I must next notice the modern Unitarians, who on some points differ from him. Where there is no acknowledged creed or catechism,[38] which may be quoted as authority, it is difficult to

---

[37] John v. 30.

[38] The following are extracts from the "Book of Common Prayer reformed," professing to have been a selection made by "the late Rev. Theophilus Lindsey for the use of the congregation in Essex Street"— and as a liturgy is generally allowed to be a fair exponent of the doctrines of those who use it—perhaps we may assume that the violent and reprehensible expressions made use of by some few persons of this persuasion, are not such as would be acknowledged by the congregations of Unitarians in general.

Form of baptism. "I baptize thee into (εἰς) the name of the Father and of the Son and of the Holy Spirit."

"Almighty and ever blessed God, by whose providence the different generations of mankind are raised up to know thee and to enjoy thy favour for ever; grant that this child now dedicated to thee as the disciple of thy Son Jesus Christ our Lord, may be endued with heavenly virtues . . . and that we may daily proceed in all virtue and goodness of living, till we come to that eternal kingdom which thou hast promised by Christ our Lord."

Order for the administration of the Lord's Supper. Confession, the same as in the liturgy of the English church as far as "we do heartily repent and are heartily sorry for these our misdoings, the remembrance of which is grievous unto us. Have mercy upon us, have mercy upon us,

give the doctrines of a sect with any precision; but as far as it is possible to judge from the writings most in repute among the Unitarians, they disclaim the notion of the miraculous conception, and believe Christ to have been to all intents and purposes *a mere man*. At the same time they allow him to have been so inspired and guided by God, that it is difficult to see where they draw the line between their own creed and that of the church, which allows the perfect humanity of Jesus, but asserts that "God and man make one Christ," namely, that the message of peace was that of God speaking by human lips, and that the Anointed prophet who declared it, was, when so anointed, the

---

most merciful Father; forgive us all that is past: and grant that we may ever hereafter serve and please thee in newness of life to the honour and glory of thy name." The absolution is the same with the trifling change of *us* for *you*. The sentences following are the same till "Hear also what St. John saith," where the text I John i. 8, 9, is substituted.

Prayer before the minister receives the communion. "Almighty God, our heavenly Father, by whose gracious assistance and for our benefit, thy beloved Son our Lord Jesus Christ, was obedient even to the death upon the cross; who did institute, and in his holy gospel command us to continue, a perpetual memorial of his death until his coming again; hear us, we most humbly beseech thee; and grant that we may receive this bread and wine in grateful remembrance of his death and sufferings, and of thy great mercy to mankind in sending him, thy chosen messenger, to turn us from darkness to light, from vice to virtue, from ignorance and error to the knowledge of thee, the only true God, whom to know is life everlasting."

Form of administration. "Take and eat this bread in remembrance of Christ"—"Take and drink this wine in remembrance of Christ."

In the daily service many prayers are omitted, so as to make the service much shorter. The exhortation and confession are the same; for the absolution is substituted "Almighty God, unto whom all hearts are open, all desires known and from whom no secrets are hid; purify the thoughts of our hearts that we may perfectly love thee, and worthily magnify thy holy name through Christ our Lord."—It would be useless to multiply extracts—enough has been given to show the doctrine of the Unitarian congregations who use this liturgy.

temple and place of manifestation of the living God. They disclaim the doctrine of atonement, and believe that the mission of Christ had for its object the reform of the world, and the restoration of man to a sense of his true relation towards God, and even here Scripture and the early church speak a language which differs not very greatly from theirs. For the language in which our redemption is spoken of, is that of a master purchasing a slave, as will be seen on a reference to Rom. vi. in the original. The ransom by which man was purchased to be the servant of holiness instead of that of sin, was paid to his former master, sin; by the purchaser; and the purchaser is God. "I speak after the manner of men," says St. Paul, "because of the infirmity of your flesh." i.e. I adopt the phraseology of a common transaction because your minds are not sufficiently accustomed to the contemplation of higher things to understand them without a metaphor; but the Unitarian forgets, when asserting that the ransom was not paid *to* God, that it was paid *by* God: and that man, the slave, was bought from sin, the master, at no less a price than the condescension of the Deity himself to the infirmity of our flesh, by making himself visibly and tangibly known to his creatures, through the medium of a human form.

have now endeavoured to give a dispassionate view of the doctrines of these sects, hitherto so much misunderstood, and having marked the points wherein they appear to me to recede from Christian truth, I have the pleasanter task before me, of showing by extracts from their writings, how large a portion of the religion which we all profess, they still retain, and I may say from experience, on most occasions conscientiously act upon.

"If with the Apostle we glory in the cross of Christ, or in that religion which could not have been confirmed without his death, let us not only be careful to govern our lives by the precepts of it in general, but more particularly be prepared to suffer what the strictest profession of it may call us to. Let us remember that our Saviour hath said, if any man will be his disciple he must "take up his cross, and follow him." That is, he must be ready to do it rather than abandon the profession of the

Gospel, or whatever the strictest purity of it may require. A true Christian is no more *of this world* than his Lord and Master was of it. With him every thing here below is but of secondary consideration, &c.—but this we must remember for our consolation, that if, in time of persecution "He that keepeth his life shall lose it," "He that loseth his life" for the profession of the Gospel "shall keep it to life eternal." "If we suffer with Christ, we shall also reign with him and be glorified together." [39]

"The truths which relate to Jesus himself are among the *most important* which the Gospel reveals. 'We preach Christ,' says the Apostle, 'warning every man and teaching every man, that we may present every man perfect in Christ Jesus.' From this passage we derive a most important sentiment, confirmed by the whole New Testament—that the great design of all the doctrines and precepts of the Gospel, is, to exalt the character,—to promote eminent purity of heart and life, to make men 'perfect as their Father in heaven is perfect.' We must preach not to make fiery partizans, and to swell the number of a sect; not to overwhelm the mind with fear, or to heat it with feverish rapture; not to form men to the decencies of life, to a superficial goodness, which will secure the admiration of mankind. All these effects fall infinitely short of the great end of the Christian ministry. We should preach that we may make men perfect Christians: perfect, not according to the standard of the world, but according to the law of Christ; perfect in heart and in life, in solitude and in society, in the great and in the common concerns of life. Here is the purpose of Christian preaching. In this, as in a common centre, all the truths of the Gospel meet; to this they all conspire; and no doctrine has an influence on salvation, any farther than it is an aid to the perfecting of our nature." [40]

"Christ is a great Saviour, as he redeems or sets free the mind, cleansing it from evil, breathing into it the love of virtue, calling forth its noblest faculties and affections, enduing it with

---

[39] Priestly's "Discourses on Various Subjects," p. 419. See also p. 14, &c. and Prefatory Discourse, p. 93.

[40] Channing's Discourse on preaching Christ.

moral power, restoring it to order, health and liberty." * * * *
"Christ has revealed to us God as the Father, and as a Father in
the noblest sense of that word. He hath revealed Him as the
author and lover of all souls, desiring to redeem all from sin, and
to impress his likeness more and more resplendently on all; as
proffering to all that best gift in the universe, his 'holy Spirit;' as
having sent his beloved Son to train us up and to introduce us to
an 'inheritance, incorruptible, undefiled, and unfading in the
heavens.'" [41]

"I confess when I can escape the deadening power of habit,
and can receive the full import of such passages as the following,
'Come unto me, all ye that labour and are heavy laden, and I will
give you rest.' 'I am come to seek and to save that which was
lost.' 'He that confesseth me before men, him will I confess
before my Father in heaven.' 'Whosoever shall be ashamed of me
before men, of him shall the Son of Man be ashamed, when he
cometh in the glory of the Father with the holy angels.' 'In my
Father's house are many mansions; I go to prepare a place for
you;' I say, when I can succeed in realizing the import of such
passages, I feel myself listening to a being, such as never before
and never since spoke in human language. I am awed by the
consciousness of greatness which these simple words express; and
when I connect this greatness with the proofs of Christ's miracles
which I gave you in a former discourse, I am compelled to speak
with the Centurion, 'Truly this was the Son of God.' [42]

"In reading the Gospels I feel myself in the presence of one
who speaks as man never spake; whose voice is not of the earth;
who speaks with a tone of reality and authority altogether his
own; who speaks of God, as conscious of his immediate presence,
as enjoying with him the intimacy of an only Son; and who speaks
of heaven, as most familiar with the higher states of being."[43]

"Go to Jesus Christ for guidance, inspiration, and strength in
your office." * * * "The privilege of communing with such a spirit

---

[41] Channing's Works. On the great purpose of Christianity.
[42] Channing's Character of Christ.
[43] Channing's Sunday School.

is so great, and the duty of going from man to Christ is so solemn, that you must spare no effort to place yourself nearer and nearer to the Divine Master." "My brother, go forth to your labours with the spirit and power of Him who first preached the Gospel to the poor."[44]

"To Jesus the conqueror of death we owe the sure hope of immortality." * * * "Is that teacher to be scorned, who in the language of conscious greatness says to us, 'I am the resurrection and the life'?"[45]

"What are we to understand by the Divinity of Christ? In the sense in which many Christians, and perhaps a majority interpret it, we do not deny it, but believe it as firmly as themselves. We believe firmly in the Divinity of Christ's mission and office, that he spoke with Divine authority, and was a bright image of the Divine perfections. We believe that God dwelt in him, manifested himself through him, taught men by him, and communicated to him his spirit without measure. We believe that Jesus Christ was the most glorious display, expression, and representative of God to mankind, so that in seeing and knowing him, we see and know the invisible Father; so that when Christ came, God visited the world and dwelt with men more conspicuously than at any former period. In Christ's words, we hear God speaking; in his miracles, we behold God acting; in his character and life, we see an unsullied image of God's purity and love."[46]

---

[44] Channing's Charge at the Ordination of Rev. R. C. Waterston.
[45] Channing On Infidelity.
[46] Channing's System of Exclusion.

LETTER IV.

WESLEYAN METHODISTS.

Towards the beginning of the last century, two young men at Oxford, the one a fellow of Lincoln College, struck by the thoughtlessness or lukewarmness of those about them, resolved to devote themselves to closer and more profitable study. They were brothers, by name John and Charles Wesley; and two other students joined them in their evening readings of the New Testament in the Greek: the elder of the brothers was at this time about twenty-six.[47] After a year of this kind of life, they admitted two or three of the pupils of the elder brother, and one of those of the younger, to their meetings; and the following year, being joined by yet more of the students, the regularity of their lives obtained for them the title of *Methodists* from those who were not inclined to follow their example.

In 1735 another name was added to their number, which has also become celebrated: this was George Whitfield of Pembroke College, then in his eighteenth year; but of him I shall have occasion to speak by and by. I shall therefore confine myself to the Wesleys. A difference of opinion on the subjects of Freewill and Predestination separated them from their younger coadjutor in 1741, and their respective friends, adopting strongly the distinctive opinions of the two, the grand division of the sect, which sprung up from their preaching, into Wesleyan or Arminian, and Whitfieldian or Calvinistic Methodists, ensued.

---

[47] John Wesley was born in 1703.

All three received holy orders according to the ceremonial of the Church of England, and Wesley never ceased to hold his spiritual mother in high estimation. "The Church of England," he says in one place, "is the purest in Christendom." But the singularity of their proceedings raised suspicion, and though both brothers continued to profess the fullest assent to the articles and liturgy of the established church, yet their manner of preaching and form of worship had something in it which led the bishops and clergy in general to consider them as verging on Sectarianism. In many places they were refused the use of the pulpit; and then, in the perhaps enthusiastic belief that they were the appointed instruments of rekindling religion in hearts where it had been dead hitherto, they began a system of field preaching.

There were at that time large districts slumbering in utter darkness and ignorance of the saving truths of the Gospel: and it was to these that the Wesleys especially directed their attention, with a success proportioned to their zeal; and had the then heads of the church availed themselves of the assistance of these earnest men in the way they might have done, by sanctioning their missionary labours among the poor and the uninstructed, the benefit would have been incalculable. But the harsh treatment [48]they met with, drove John Wesley at last into complete schism: and then the ambition, which had perhaps animated his first exertions almost unknown to himself, assumed a bolder flight,

---

[48] "I rode over to a neighbouring town," says Wesley, "to wait upon a justice of peace, a man of candour and understanding; before whom I was informed their angry neighbours had carried a whole waggon load of these new heretics." But when he asked, "what they had done," there was a deep silence, for that was a point their conductor had forgot. At length one said, "Why they pretend to be better than other people, and besides they pray from morning till night." Mr. S--- asked, "But have they done nothing besides?" "Yes, Sir," said an old man, "an't please your worship they have *convarted* my wife; till she went among them she had such a tongue, and now she is as quiet as a lamb." "Carry them back," replied the justice, "and let them convert all the scolds in the town."—(Wesley's Journal.)

and he aspired to the distinction of being the head and leader of a sect which grew so rapidly, that at the time of his death in 1791, "the number of members in connexion with him in Europe, America, and the West Indian Islands, was 80,000. And at the last conference in 1831 the numbers returned were, in Great Britain, 249,119; in Ireland, 22,470; in the Foreign Missions, 42,743. Total 314,332. Exclusive of more than half a million of persons in the Societies in the States of America." [49]

You are probably aware that, besides the public preaching, Wesley instituted among his people several kinds of private meetings. To the public prayer meetings, which were generally held in private houses, persons not of this sect were often invited, and on these occasions a hymn was first sung, then they all knelt, and the first who felt "moved" made an extempore prayer: when he had finished, another commenced, and so on for about two hours. These prayer meetings were held in such high esteem among the Methodists, that they asserted more were "born again" and "made free," as they termed it, "from all the remains of sin" than at any other meetings, public preachings, &c.

There was much in this kind of meeting which was likely to lead to enthusiasm, which is universally found to be most easily awakened where numbers are congregated; and according to an author formerly of their persuasion,[50] the consequence was such as might have been expected. "It is impossible," says he, "to form any just idea of those assemblies except you had been present at them. One coaxes the Divine Being, another is amorous, and a third will tell the Deity, 'He must be a liar if he does not grant all they ask.' They thus go on working up each other's imagination until they become as it were spiritually intoxicated, and while in this state they sometimes recollect a text or two of Scripture, such as 'Thy sins are forgiven thee'—'Go and sin no more'—'Go in peace,' &c. and then declare themselves to be 'born again' or 'sanctified.'"

---

[49] Watson's Life of Wesley, page 484.
[50] Lackington.

The love feast is also a private meeting of as many members of the community as choose to attend; and they generally assemble from all parts within several miles of the place where the feast is held. They then alternately sing and pray, and some among them, who think that their experience, as they term it, is remarkable, stand up, and narrate all the transactions which they say have taken place between God, the devil, and their souls.

There is a curious propensity to egotism in human nature which frequently shews itself in religious matters. Men love to talk of themselves: and the Romanist finds pleasure in the power of pouring forth all his feelings and thoughts to his father confessor, whenever he is strongly excited by passion: of this I have become aware from personal knowledge. Other enthusiasts enjoy no less satisfaction in talking of the interior conflicts they have sustained; for all ungoverned feeling loves to vent itself in speech, and the lover who talks of his mistress, or the penitent who talks of his sins, is for the time being in the same state of restless excitement. *Governed* feeling, on the contrary, as far as my experience goes, is silent.

In these Love Feasts those present have buns to eat, which are mutually broken between each "Brother and Sister," and water to drink, which they hand from one to another. These meetings commence about seven o'clock, and last till nine or ten.

Each society is divided into smaller companies called "classes" according to their respective places of abode. There are about twelve persons in every class, one of whom is styled "the Leader," whose business it is to see each person in his class, at least once a week, to advise, comfort, or exhort, as occasion may require, and to receive what each is willing to give towards the support of the Gospel.

It is expected that every member should continue to evince his desire of salvation by abstaining from "the taking of the name of the Lord in vain"; "the profaning of the Lord's day, either by ordinary work thereon, or by buying and selling"; "drunkenness, buying or selling spirituous liquors, or drinking them, unless in cases of extreme necessity; fighting, quarreling, brawling; going to law with a brother; returning evil for evil, or railing for railing; the using many words in buying or selling.[51] The buying or selling uncustomed goods; the giving or taking things on usury, i.e. unlawful interest; the putting on of gold or costly apparel; the taking such diversions as cannot be used in the name of the Lord Jesus Christ; the singing those songs or reading those books, that do not tend to the knowledge or love of God;—softness and needless self-indulgence, &c.[52]

Among the duties expected and required of the members are all kinds of beneficence, diligence, frugality,[53] self-denial, and attendance on all the ordinances of God, among which is specifically mentioned fasting. If any member habitually break any of these rules he is admonished; and if he do not then repent, expulsion follows. "Marrying with unbelievers," and bankruptcy, if the party has not kept fair accounts, are also followed by expulsion.

No one I think can doubt that much good was effected by the first preaching of Wesley and his disciples, for at that time our church was in a lethargic state, and the lower orders shamefully neglected in spiritual matters in many parts of

---

[51] "Who does as he would be done by, in buying or selling? particularly selling horses? Write him a knave that does not, and the Methodist knave is the worst of all knaves."—*Wesley's Large Minutes*, Q. 13.

[52] Snuff-taking and drams are expressly forbidden.

[53] In May 1776, an order was made in the House of Lords, "That the Commissioners of His Majesty's Excise do write circular letters to all such persons whom they have reason to suspect to have plate, as also to those who have not paid regularly the duty on the same." In consequence of this order the Accountant-general for household plate sent a copy of it to John Wesley. The answer was as follows:

Sir,

I have *two* silver teaspoons in London and two at Bristol: this is all the plate which I have at present, and I shall not buy any more while so many round me want bread.

I am Sir, your most humble servant,
John Wesley.

England. Yet there are some things which excite one's regret in their practices, and of these none displeases me more than the familiar use of Scripture language, which when properly and judiciously applied is striking and solemn; but to hear every notion of enthusiastic ignorance, every rise and fall of the animal spirits, expressed in the language of the Apostles and Evangelists, and even of our Lord himself; to witness their familiarity with the Almighty, their full trust and confidence in the reality of small miracles wrought at their request;—must always be painful to a soberly religious mind. In a book entitled "The Bank of Faith," the author asserts, that a dog brought him mutton to eat, that fish died at night in a pond on purpose to be eaten by him in the morning, and that money, clothes, &c. in short every thing he could desire he attained by prayer. [54]

An old woman of Wesley's society, named Mary Hubbard, would often wash her linen, hang it out to dry, and go away to work in the fields or to Taunton Market four miles from her house, and when blamed for thus leaving her linen unprotected, she would reply that "the Lord watched over her and all that she had, and that he would prevent any person from stealing her two old smocks, or if He permitted them to be stolen, He would send her two new ones in their stead." I seriously assure you, says the author who relates this tale, and who at one time went even greater lengths[55] than this old woman, "that there are many thousand Mary Hubbards among the Methodists."

---

[54] "I used my prayers," says the author of the 'Bank of Faith,' "*as gunners do swivels; turning them every way* as the cases required." Wesley relates in his Journal that "By prayer he used to cure a violent pain in his head," &c.

[55] This writer, the celebrated Lackington the bookseller, relates the following occurrence soon after he turned Methodist. "One Sunday morning at eight o'clock, my mistress seeing her sons set off, and knowing they were gone to a Methodist meeting, determined to prevent me from doing the same, by locking the door; on which in a superstitious mood I opened the Bible for direction what to do, and the first words I read were these, "He shall give his angels charge

It may be added, that their strict abstinence from the common amusements of the world, even where innocent in themselves, has its evils, as I have already noticed when speaking of the Quakers; for the mind cannot always be kept in a state of tension, and if we refuse ourselves recreation altogether, there is danger that we shall find the yoke of Christ a wearisome instead of an easy one, and cast it off in disgust; nay, I am afraid that if we were to inquire closely, we should find instances enough of this result to demonstrate, what indeed wants but little proof, i.e. that God knows better than we do "whereof we are made," and that it is not wisdom to bind a heavy burthen on our shoulders when Christ himself has declared that his is light. Still, though tinged with a degree of enthusiasm which we may regret, the doctrine of the Wesleyan Methodists retains the fundamental parts of Christianity, and after reading the following extracts from Wesley's Sermons, I think you will hardly forbear asking, Why is this a separate sect?

"Justifying Faith implies not only a Divine ελεγχος, evidence or conviction, that 'God was in Christ reconciling the world to himself,' but a sure trust and confidence that Christ died for *my* sins, that he loved *me*, and gave himself for me; and the moment a penitent sinner believes this, God pardons and absolves him."[56] "Christian perfection does not imply, as some men seem

concerning thee, lest at any time thou dash thy foot against a stone." This was enough for me, so without a moment's hesitation I ran up two pair of stairs to my own room, and out of the window I leapt to the great terror of my poor mistress. My feet and ancles were most intolerably bruised, so that I was obliged to be put to bed; and it was more than a month before I recovered the use of my limbs. I was then ignorant enough to think that *the Lord had not used me very well*; and I resolved *not to put so much trust in him* for the future. My rash adventure made a great noise in the town, and was talked of many miles round. Some few admired my prodigious strength of faith; but the major part pitied me as a poor ignorant, deluded, and infatuated boy."

[56] Wesley's Works, vol. xii. p. 49. Some of Wesley's expressions, when confronted with each other, appear incompatible; in such cases the main

to have imagined, an exemption either from ignorance, or mistake, or infirmities, or temptations; indeed it is only another term for holiness: thus every one that is holy, is in the Scripture sense 'perfect.' We may yet observe that neither in this respect is there absolute perfection on earth."[57] "If the Scriptures are true, those who are holy or religious in the judgment of God himself, those who are endued with the faith that purifies the heart, that produces a good conscience; those who live by faith in the Son of God; those who are sanctified by the blood of the Covenant may nevertheless so fall from God as to perish everlastingly, therefore let him who thinketh he standeth take heed lest he fall." "In strictness neither our faith nor our works justify us, i.e. *deserve* the remission of our sins, but God himself justifies us of his own mercy through the merits of his Son only." [58]

---

drift of the writer must always be considered; for it is much more usual to fail in expressing our meaning than to express contradictory opinions: since the latter implies a cerebral defect verging on insanity, the former merely results from a faulty style. Scripture does not any where warrant us in saying "*the moment* a penitent sinner," &c.; but requires from us a proof of this belief by actions conformable to it. God has promised us immortality through his Son, only if we not merely believe, but "do that which is lawful and right."

[57] Wesley censured some of his preachers for pushing the doctrine of perfection too far.

[58] Wesley's Works, vol. viii. p. 219. and vol. xi. p. 415.

LETTER V.

GENERAL BAPTISTS, MORAVIANS, SWEDENBORGIANS, PLYMOUTH BRETHREN.

Among the sects which arose about the period of the Reformation of the church in the sixteenth century, we find the Anabaptists[59] playing rather a conspicuous part, by exciting political tumults in Saxony and the adjacent countries. For this, Munzer, their leader, after the defeat of his forces, was put to death, and the sect generally was proscribed, and the profession of its doctrines punished capitally. What those doctrines were is not easy, nor is it essential now, to state, since the modern sect, which we now term Baptists, retain only so much of them as relates to baptism by immersion, and of adults only, and the rejection of episcopal church government.

The more modern sect is subdivided into General and Particular Baptists. The General or Arminian Baptists admit "much latitude in their system of religious doctrine, which consists in such general principles, that their communion is accessible to Christians of almost all denominations, and

---

[59] So called from their habit of rebaptizing those who entered their communion. They were afterwards called *Antipædobaptists*, from their objection to *pædo* or infant baptism; and finally, the English habit of abbreviation of words at all commonly used, contracted the word into *Baptist.*

accordingly they tolerate in fact, and receive among them persons of every sect, who profess themselves Christians, and receive the Holy Scriptures as the source of truth, and the rule of faith." [60]They agree with the Particular Baptists in this, that they admit to baptism adults only, and administer that sacrament either by dipping or total immersion; but they differ from them in another respect, for they repeat the administration of baptism to those who had received it, either in a state of infancy, or by aspersion instead of dipping: for if the common accounts may be believed, the Particular Baptists do not carry matters so far.

The General Baptists consider their sect as the only true church; in baptism they dip only once and not three times as was the practice in the primitive church: and they consider it a matter of indifference whether that sacrament be administered in the name of Father, Son, and Holy Ghost, or in that of Christ alone:[61] they adopt the doctrine of Menno with regard to the Millennium; many of them also embrace his particular opinion concerning the origin of Christ's body.[62] They look upon the precept of the Apostles prohibiting the use of blood and of things strangled, as a law that was designed to be in force in all ages and periods of the church: they believe that the soul, from the moment that the body dies until its resurrection at the last day, remains in a state of perfect insensibility: they use the ceremony of extreme unction, and finally, to omit matters of a more trifling nature, several of them observe the Jewish as well as the Christian Sabbath.[63] In some of their churches they have three distinct orders separately ordained, i.e. messengers, elders, and deacons; and their general assembly (where a minister preaches, and the churches are taken into consideration), is held annually in London on the Tuesday in

---

[60] Mosheim. Ecc. Hist. Cant. XVI. Sect, iii. Part 2.

[61] Milton belonged to the class of Anti-Trinitarian General Baptists.

[62] That the body of Jesus was not derived from the substance of the blessed Virgin, but created in her womb by an omnipotent act of the Holy Spirit.

[63] V. Mosheim's Ecc. Hist.

Whitsun week, and they afterwards dine together. They have met thus for upwards of a century.

The propriety of the exclusive application of the term "Baptists" to those who baptize adults by immersion, has been questioned; and for this reason they are by many styled Antipædobaptists,[64] namely, opposers of infant baptism; but the term Anabaptist should not be applied to them, it being a term of reproach.

The old General Baptists have been on the decline for many years; their churches are principally in Kent and Sussex. The English and most foreign Baptists consider a personal profession of faith, and immersion in water, essential to baptism: this profession is generally made before the church at a church meeting. Some have a creed, and expect the candidate for baptism to assent to it, and give a circumstantial account of his conversion: others only require him to profess himself a Christian. The former generally consider baptism as an ordinance which initiates persons into a particular church, and they say, that without breach of Christian liberty, they have a right to expect an agreement in articles of faith in their own societies. The latter think that baptism initiates into the Christian religion generally, and therefore think that they have no right to require an assent to their creed from such as do not join their churches. They quote the baptism of the Eunuch in Acts viii. in proof.

The first mention of the Baptists in English History is as the subject of persecution in the reign of Henry VIII. During that of Edward VI. a commission was issued to bishops and other persons "to try all Anabaptists, heretics, and despisers of the common prayer," and they were empowered, in the event of their contumacy, to commit them to the flames. The same inhuman policy was persisted in under Elizabeth. The last Baptist martyr burned in England was Edward Wightman; he was condemned by

---

[64] All who baptize infants may be termed pædo-baptists; the word is derived from the Greek πάις a child or infant, and βάπτω to baptize.

the bishop of Lichfield and Coventry,[65] and burned at Lichfield April 11, 1612.[66]

The celebrated Whiston became a Baptist towards the close of his life, retaining nevertheless his Arian belief.

The Moravians are supposed to have derived their origin from Nicholas Lewis, Count Zinzendorf, a German nobleman, who died in 1760. The society however assert that they are descended from the old Moravian and Bohemian Brethren, who existed as a distinct sect sixty years prior to the Reformation. No sooner had these Moravian Brethren heard of Luther's bold testimony to the truth, and of the success which attended his labours, than they sent in the year 1522 two deputies to assure him of "the deep interest which they took in his work;" giving him, at the same time, an account of their own doctrine and constitution. They were most kindly received; and both Luther, and his colleague Bucer, recognised the Moravians as holding the same faith; and bore honourable testimony to the purity of their doctrine, and the excellence of their discipline. The chief doctrine of the Moravian society is, that "by the sacrifice for sin made by Jesus Christ, and by that alone, grace and deliverance from sin are to be obtained for all mankind:" and they stedfastly maintain the following points:

1. The divinity of Christ.

2. The atonement and satisfaction made for us by Jesus Christ; and that by his merits alone we receive freely the forgiveness of sin, and sanctification in soul and body.

3. The doctrine of the Holy Spirit, and the operations of his grace. That it is he who worketh in us conviction of sin, faith in Christ, and pureness of heart.

4. That faith must evidence itself by willing obedience to the commandments of God from love and gratitude.

---

[65] Yet the bishop ought to have known that baptism by immersion was practised in the church for many centuries, and the rubric of our common prayer leaves the option of immersion or aspersion.
[66] Condor's View. p. 380.

The internal constitution of the ancient church of the Moravians, which is still substantially adhered to, was originally adopted in 1457, and more definitely settled in 1616 by the Synod of Zerawitz. Its principal peculiarities are,

1. Every church is divided into three classes, i.e. 1. *Beginners* or *Catechumens*. 2. *The more advanced* or *communicants*, who are considered as members of the church. 3. *The perfect*, consisting of such as have persevered for some time in a course of true piety. From this last class are chosen in every church *the Elders*, from three to eight in number.

2. Every congregation is directed by a board of elders, whose province it is to have a watchful eye over its members with respect to the doctrine and deportment. Once in three months these elders are bound to visit the houses of the brethren, in order to observe their conduct, and to ascertain whether every one is labouring diligently in his calling, &c. of which they make a report to the pastor. They also are required to visit the sick, and assist the poorer brethren with money, contributed by the members of the church, and deposited in an alms box.

3. The ministration of the Word and Sacrament is performed either by members who have received ordination from the bishops of the church of the brethren, or by those who have received that of the Calvinist or Lutheran church. The deacons, according to the ancient constitution of the church, are the chief assistants of the pastors, and are considered as candidates for the ministry. The bishops, who are nominated by the ministers, appoint the pastors to their stations, and have the power of removing them when they think fit, and of ordaining the deacons as well as the ministers. Every bishop is appointed to superintend a certain number of churches, and has two or three co-bishops, who, if necessary, supply their place. The ancient church appointed some of its members to the business of watching over the civil affairs of the congregation, under the name of *Seniores Civiles*, who were ordained with imposition of hands. This office is still continued. The synods, which are held every three or four years, are composed of the bishops and their co-bishops the

Seniores Civiles, and of "such servants of the church and of the congregation as are called to the synod by the former elders' conference, appointed by the previous synod, or commissioned to attend it as deputies from particular congregations." Several female elders also are usually present at the synods, but they have no vote. All the transactions of the synod are committed to writing, and communicated to the several congregations.

A liturgy, peculiar to the Brethren, is regularly used as a part of the morning service on the Sabbath; on other occasions the minister offers extempore prayer. The singing of hymns is considered as an essential part of worship, and many of their services consist entirely of singing. At the baptism of children, both the witnesses and the minister bless the infant, with laying on of hands immediately after the rite. The Lord's Supper is celebrated every month: love feasts are frequently held, i.e. the members eat and drink together in fellowship: cakes and tea are distributed during the singing of some verses by the congregation. The washing of feet is practised at present only at certain seasons by the whole congregation, and on some other occasions in the choirs. Dying persons are blessed for their departure by the elders, during prayer and singing a verse with imposition of hands. At funerals, the pastor accompanies the corpse to the burial place with the singing of hymns; and an address is delivered at the grave. Marriages are, by general agreement, never contracted without the advice and concurrence of the elders.[67] The casting of lots is used among them to know, as they express it, "The will of the Lord."[68]

With regard to discipline, "the Church of the Brethren have agreed upon certain rules and orders. These are laid before every one, that desires to become a member of the church, for his consideration. Whoever after having voluntarily agreed to them, does not act conformably, falls under congregation discipline." This has various degrees, and consists in admonitions, warnings, and reproofs, continued until genuine repentance and a real conversion become evident in the offender, when he is readmitted to the holy communion, or reconciled to the congregation, after a deprecatory letter has been read, expressing the offender's sorrow for his transgression, and asking forgiveness. The Brethren assert that the church government in the established Protestant churches "does not apply to the congregations of the Brethren, because they never were intended to form a national establishment: for their design is no other than to be a true and living congregation of Jesus Christ, and to build up each other as a spiritual house of God, to the end that the kingdom of Jesus Christ may be furthered by them." Hence the doctrine of Jesus and his Apostles, and the order and practice of the Apostolic churches, are the models by which they wish to be formed. It may be added, that they are generally the most successful Missionaries, and that their society seems the most nearly to realize the practice of the early Christians, of any sect now remaining.

---

[67] Marriage is enumerated in one of the Moravian hymns amongst the services of danger, for which the United Brethren are "to hold themselves prepared."
"You as yet single are but little tried,
Invited to the supper of the bride,
That like the former warrior each may stand
Ready for land, sea, marriage, at command."

[68] See Latrobe's edition of Spangenburgh's Exposition of Christian Doctrine.

The Swedenborgians take their name from Emmanuel Swedenborg, who was born at Stockholm in 1683. His father was Jasper Swedberg, bishop of West Gothland. He received his education chiefly in the University of Upsala; and in 1716 was appointed by Charles XII. Assessor of the Royal College of Sciences; he was ennobled by Queen Ulrica Eleonora, and received the name of Swedenborg. He published scientific works on various subjects, but in 1747 he resigned his office, in order, as he himself states, that he might be more at liberty to attend to that new function which he considered himself called to, and the rest of his life was spent in composing and publishing the voluminous works which contain his peculiar doctrines. He died in 1772. He was a man of blameless life and amiable deportment, and was distinguished for his attainments in mathematics and mechanics.

His writings are so very obscure, that it is difficult to state what are the opinions contained in them; he taught, however, that by the New Jerusalem which came down from heaven, was intended a new church as to doctrine, and that he was the person to whom this doctrine was revealed, and who was appointed to make it known to the world. Swedenborg made no attempt to found a sect; but after his death, his followers, in 1788, formed themselves into a society under the denomination of "The New Jerusalem Church." They have several places of meeting, both in London and Manchester, and send delegates to a "General Conference," under whose direction a liturgy has been prepared, from which I shall make a few extracts to shew the peculiar doctrines of this sect.

The following are some of the questions asked of the candidate for ordination, which is performed by imposition of hands, of course of a minister of their own communion.

"*Min.* Dost thou believe that Jehovah God is One both in Essence and in Person; in whom, nevertheless, is the Divine Trinity of Father, Son, and Holy Spirit; and that these are, his Essential Divinity, his Divine Humanity, and his Divine Proceeding, which are the three Essentials of One God, answering to the soul, the body, and the operative energy, in man, and that the Lord and Saviour Jesus Christ is that God?

Dost thou believe that by his temptations, the last of which was the passion of the cross, the Lord united, in his Humanity, Divine Truth to Divine Good, or Divine Wisdom to Divine Love, and so returned into his Divinity in which he was from eternity, together with, and in, his Glorified Humanity?

Dost thou believe that the sacred Scripture, or Word of God, is Divine Truth itself, and that it contains a spiritual and celestial sense, heretofore unknown, whence it is divinely inspired and holy in every syllable; as well as a literal sense, which is the basis and support of its spiritual and celestial sense?

Dost thou believe that the books which have the internal sense and are truly the Word of God are,—the five books of Moses, Joshua, Judges, the two books of Samuel, the two books of Kings, the Psalms of David, the prophets, including the Lamentations of Jeremiah, the four Gospels, and the Revelation[69]?"

It is further stated in their eleventh article of faith, "That immediately after death, which is only a putting off of the material body, never to be resumed, man rises again in a spiritual or substantial body, in which he continues to live to eternity."

On these doctrines it may be observed that the forms of worship founded on them are not such as Christ and his apostles ordered. The doxology is, "To Jesus Christ be glory and dominion for ever and ever;" the blessing, "The grace of our Lord Jesus Christ be with you all." The prayers are addressed to the "blessed Lord Jesus." Whereas Christ, when he gave us a form of prayer, bade us address "our Father in heaven;" and bade us ask of the Father in his name; and the form of the apostolic doxology is, "To God only wise be glory through Jesus Christ for ever"; [70]and the blessing, "Grace be unto you and peace from God our Father, and from the Lord Jesus Christ."[71] As at this time Christ had

---

[69] Litany of the New Church. Office of ordination, p. 151.

[70] Rom. xxi. 27.

[71] I Cor. i. 3.

ascended from the earth, had the human nature been entirely merged in the Divine, as this sect asserts, Paul the Apostle would not have made this distinction, which implies that the Lord Jesus still existed somewhere in his human form as the everlasting visible temple of the Invisible father of all things, for "no man hath seen God at any time," says the beloved Apostle,[72] and this is confirmed by Christ himself.[73] If the man then be lost in the Deity, it follows that the Lord Jesus exists no more for us. I am aware that this consequence is denied by the sect, but it is a self evident proposition: for their creed runs thus, "I believe in one God in whom is a Divine Trinity, &c., and that this God is the Lord and Saviour Jesus Christ who is Jehovah in a glorified human form." Now a human form must have some properties of matter; it must be visible, and circumscribed, or it is not form; and what is circumscribed and visible cannot be God, who, of necessity, is uncircumscribed, and therefore invisible. The infinite Eternal Omnipotent Deity *must* be where that glorified body is not; therefore, the Great Father of all things must always be the object of worship, through Jesus Christ, who is the *visible* image of his glory. The *form* of baptism is retained by this sect, though they assert that the rite was "constantly administered by the Apostles in the name of Christ alone"; an assertion contradicted by the whole testimony of antiquity from the earliest times; adding, "nevertheless it is well to use the express words of the Lord, when it is known and acknowledged in the church that the Father and the Son and the Holy Spirit are not three separate persons but three Divine Essentials, constituting the single Divine Person of our Lord Jesus Christ."[74] With regard to the "internal sense" of Scripture it is sufficient to observe that if "every syllable" were to be considered as inspired and holy, the long list of various readings would grievously shake our faith, though these are quite immaterial as to the general meaning.

---

[72] John i. 18.
[73] John vi. 46.
[74] Liturgy of the New Church Office of Baptism, p. 58.

There are serious objections to the distinctive tenets of this sect, yet, in justice to them, it must be allowed that the unguarded language of some preachers does so split up the Deity into separate individuals as to make the doctrine so taught a complete tritheism, and that a serious mind returning to the express declaration of the Scripture, that God is One, may be so far shocked by such unmeasured expressions, as to run into the extreme which I have condemned. Unitarianism on the one hand, and the doctrine of Swedenborg on the other, have equally sprung from a want of proper caution when speaking of the different manifestations of the Deity, and an unmeasured itch for the definition of things too far beyond the reach of our finite faculties to admit of any precision of terms. *Words* were formed for the things pertaining to earth; how then can they ever exactly express the nature of the Deity?

Notwithstanding the faith professed by this sect, their teaching, nevertheless, returns to the doctrine of the Gospel. In a tract "on the true meaning of the intercession of Jesus Christ," published at Manchester by their own religious tract society, we have the following passage: "The Humanity named Jesus is the medium whereby man may come to God, because the Father, *heretofore invisible*, is manifested and made *visible* and *approachable* in him. This is meant by *our coming unto God by him*;" and elsewhere, as we cannot obtain this "light of life" without following the Lord, and doing his will, as he did the will of the Father, agreeably to his own saying, "If ye keep my commandments, even as I have kept my Father's commandments, and abide in his love;" so neither can we obtain that divine food by which our spiritual life is to be sustained, unless we labour for it, as the Lord himself instructed us when he said "Labour for the meat which endureth unto everlasting life"; and is it not of the greatest importance clearly to understand what this labour implies? Let the reader be assured that he must labour in that spiritual vineyard which the Lord desires to plant in his soul, in order that it may bear abundant fruits of righteousness to the glory of his heavenly father."[75] Thus we see again that the fundamental doctrines of Christianity *will* find their way, however men may speculatively disclaim them. Why then do we differ outwardly, when at heart we agree?

The Plymouth Brethren, so called probably from the place where this society first arose, do not allow themselves to be a sect, though in their practices they differ considerably from those of the Established Church. They meet together on the morning of the first day of the week to celebrate the Lord's Supper, when any "Brother" is at liberty to speak for mutual edification. In the afternoon and evening, when they have preachers, the services are similar to those in the Congregational Churches (Independents): the desk, however, for they condemn pulpits, is not occupied by one man, but used as a convenient place for speaking, being alternately occupied by the "Brother," who reads the hymn, the one who prays, and the one who teaches or preaches the Word. There are also "Meetings for Prayer," and what are technically called "reading meetings;" when a chapter is read, and those "Brethren" who have made it matter of reflection, speak upon it clause by clause for their mutual instruction.

Before a person is acknowledged a "Brother," his name is announced at one of the times of "meeting together to break bread," as it is termed, and if nothing occurs in the interval, he takes his seat with them the next Sunday.[76] Any one is admitted to their communion whom they believe to be "a child of God;" but they do not receive or acknowledge him as a brother, "while in actual connection with any of the various forms of worldliness," i.e. the other churches of Christ. Their preachers move about from place to place, forming different congregations, which they again leave for other places where their services are required. None of their ministers receive any *stipulated* charity. The "Brethren" disapprove of any association of Christians for any purpose whatever, whether civil or religious, and therefore discountenance all Sunday School, Bible, Missionary, or even

[75] "Jesus the Fountain of Life and Light," p. 12.
[76] In some places it is not till the end of a fortnight.

purely Benevolent, Societies. They do not disapprove of sending either Bibles or Missionaries to the heathen; but they say that if they go at all, "God and not the church must send them." They do not think that the Gospel is to convert the world, but that it is to be "preached as a witness to" or rather against "all nations." The world, they say, "is reserved for judgment, and therefore it is wholly contrary to the character of a Christian to have any thing to do with it or its government." When a child of God is born again, "he lays," say they, "all his worldly relations down at the feet of Christ, and he is at liberty to take up none but those which he can take up in the Lord." They neither pray for pardon of sin, nor for the presence and influence of the Spirit, and carefully exclude such petitions from their hymns. Many of them think it inconsistent with the Christian character to amass wealth, or to possess furniture or clothing more than is *necessary* for health and cleanliness; and very great sacrifices have been made by the more wealthy of them.

These are most of them unimportant peculiarities; but the great feature of this sect, for so notwithstanding their protest, I must call these "Brethren," is a degree of self approbation and uncharity for others, which, to say the least, is not what Christ taught. "No sect," says Rust,[77] "is more Sectarian, and none more separate from Christians of all denominations than "The Plymouth Brethren." The Church of Rome they consider "bad." The Church of England "bad." "A popish priest and a parish priest, both bad;" "but infinitely worse," says one of the Brethren (a Captain Hall), "is a people's preacher." They occasionally indulge in what they term "biting jests and sarcastic raillery," of the ministers of our church, and of those who differ from them, which evince but little of the meek and peaceable spirit of the Gospel;[78] for, as Lord Bacon has well observed, "to intermix

---

[77] Examination of the opinions of the Plymouth Brethren.

[78] The following is a sample from one of their published works: "The first eclogue of Virgil has always appeared to me to express most felicitously the pleasures of a *pastoral* life as we too frequently see it in these days. With what force the following lines describe the grateful

Scripture with scurrility in one sentence;—the majesty of religion and the contempt and deformity of things ridiculous,—is a thing far from the reverence of a devout Christian, and hardly becoming the honest regard of a sober man." If I have appeared to speak harshly of this sect, it is because they seem to me to have abandoned so much of the spirit of the Gospel. "If the tenets of the Plymouth Brethren be consistent with themselves," observes Mr. Rust, "they necessarily withdraw them from all society, and every existing form of Christianity, shutting them out from all co-operation with the holy and benevolent, for the relief and blessing of their poor or sinful fellow creatures, making it sinful to fulfil the duties of a subject, a citizen, &c." But I hope and believe that these tenets must be and are counteracted by the instinctive love of our kind, which for the benefit of the world God has implanted in man. The human race is so essentially social that they who endeavour to dissociate mankind, stand in much the

---

feeling of a *young clergyman*, who is recounting the benefits conferred on him by his patron:

O Meliboee, Deus nobis hæc otia fecit.
Namque erit ille mihi semper Deus—
Ille meas errare boves, ut cernis, et ipsum
Ludere, qæe vellem, calamo permisit agresti.

My patron shall always be a divinity to me, for he put me into this life of ease when he gave me this *gem, the prettiest living in England.* He gave me this *easy duty,* so that I can let my flock wander wheresoever it may please them, as you see they do; while I myself do just what I like, and occasionally amuse myself with a *pianoforte* by Stoddart, that cost eighty-five guineas."

"He (the congregational minister) is now, in his own opinion, the one man of the whole body of believers in all the services of the sanctuary. He utters all their sentiments of faith and doctrine, and offers up all their prayers! How can he justify the position he has assumed as *an usurper?* yea as a *grievous wolf!* in that he has swallowed up *all the gifts of the Holy Ghost* in the *voracity of his selfishness,*" &c. It is not thus that the "unity of the church," which they profess to desire is likely to be cemented.

same situation as he would do who should hope to dam up the ocean. It is in fact to these silent tendencies of human nature, whose force we never know till we attempt to check them, that we owe much of the innocuousness of false or overstrained opinions: the reason is deluded, but the feelings which the Creator has made a part of our very being, generally correct the false argument; and the man, if not previously corrupted by vice, acts right though he argues wrong.

LETTER VI.

CALVINISM.

I have already noticed that the sects into which the reformed churches are split, may be classified generally under two great divisions, the one adopting mainly the milder views of Melancthon, whose advice was much used in the reform of the Anglican church; the other following those of Calvin, which were chiefly carried out, at Geneva, the birthplace of that reformer, and among the Huguenots of France. It may be well, therefore, before we proceed to notice the particular sects which profess to combine in a greater or less degree the doctrines usually termed Calvinistic, to examine what the opinions are which pass under that name. [79]

It was at the Synod of Dort, which was assembled in the year 1618, that these opinions received a decided form; for James Arminius, professor of divinity in the University of Leyden, having rejected some part of the Genevan doctrine respecting predestination and grace, this synod was called in order to settle the disputed points. After much debate the opinions of Arminius were condemned, and the doctrine of Calvin was summed up in five points, which gave name to what has been called the

---

[79] Bishop Jewel, in his "Defence of his apology for the Church of England," says, that "the term *Calvinist* was in the first instance applied to the Reformers and the English Protestants as a matter of reproach by the Church of Rome."

Quinqueticular controversy between the Calvinistic and Anti-calvinistic divines of Holland. They related to,

1. Predestination or Election.
2. The extent of redemption.
3. Moral depravity and impotency. [80]
4. Effectual calling.
5. Final perseverance of the sanctified.

Calvinists are understood to maintain that predestination is absolute; redemption limited; moral impotency total; grace inevitable; and the salvation of the believer, certain. But among Calvinistic as among Arminian divines, there are many shades of difference indicated by the terms *high* Calvinist, and *moderate* Calvinist, *sub* lapsarian and *supra* lapsarian, *scholastic* Calvinism and *popular* Calvinism; which latter has been described as "the Augustinian theology strained off from its mathematics." These all differ so materially that Bishop Horsley found it necessary to admonish his clergy "to beware how they aimed their shaft at Calvinism before they knew what it is, and what it is not;" a great part of what ignorantly goes under that name, being "closely interwoven with the very rudiments of Christianity." I believe, however, that though differences may subsist among Calvinists themselves, as to the explication of their doctrines, they generally allow,

1. That God has chosen a certain number in Christ, to everlasting glory before the foundation of the world, according to his immutable purpose, and of his free grace and love; without the least foresight of faith, good works, or any conditions performed by the creature; and that the rest of mankind he was pleased to pass by, and ordain them to dishonour and wrath for their sins to the praise of his vindictive justice.

2. That Christ by his death and sufferings made an atonement only for the sins of the elect. [81]

---

[80] Whatever difference may have subsisted between Luther and Calvin on the subject of Divine decrees, no language can be stronger than that in which Luther insists upon the moral impotence of man's depraved nature in opposition to the Pelagian doctrine of freewill.

3. That mankind are *totally* depraved in consequence of the fall.

4. That all whom God has predestined to life, he is pleased in his appointed time effectually to call by his Word and Spirit out of that state of sin and death in which they are by nature, to grace and salvation by Jesus Christ.

5. That those whom God has effectually called and sanctified by his Spirit, shall never finally fall from a state of grace.

The prominent feature then, of the Calvinistic system, [82]is the election of some, and reprobation of others from all eternity;

---

[81] It is difficult to reconcile this doctrine with 2 Cor. v. 14, 15. I Tim. ii. 6. 2 Pet. iii. 9. Rom. viii. 32. I Tim. iv. 10. &c.

[82] The best account of their system is to be found in "The Assembly's Catechism," which is taught their children. To this sect belongs more particularly the doctrine of *Atonement*, or, "that Christ by his death made satisfaction to the Divine justice for the *Elect*, appeasing the anger of the Divine Being, and effecting on his part a reconciliation." That thus Christ had, as they term it, "the sin of the Elect laid upon him." But some of their teachers do not hold this opinion, but consider Christ's death as simply a medium through which God has been pleased to exercise mercy towards the penitent. "The sacrifice of Christ," says Dr. Magee, "was never deemed by any (who did not wish to calumniate the doctrine of atonement), to have made God placable: but merely viewed as the means appointed by Divine wisdom by which to bestow forgiveness." To this it may be further added, that the language used throughout the Epistles of St. Paul with regard to the redemption of man, is that of the then familiar slave market. Man is "bought with a price" from his former master, Sin, for the service of God. The scholar who will consult Romans vi. will see immediately that all the metaphors used are those of purchase for military service; "Your members," says he, ver. 13, "shall not be the arms (ὅπλα) of unrighteousness used for the service of sin; but the arms (ὅπλα) of righteousness for God." And ver 23, τὰ γὰρ ὀψώνια τῆς ἁμαρτίας· θάνατος· τὸ δὲ χάρισμα τοῦ θεοῦ, ζωὴ, αἰώνιος ἐν Χριτῷ Ιησοῦ τῷ κυρίῳ ἡμῶν. i.e. The rations of sin are death, but the donative of God is eternal life, by means of Jesus Christ our Lord. It is impossible to express more clearly

but to this we may answer, that if all mankind are really appointed to sin and punishment, holiness and salvation irrespectively to any act of their own, then they will be judged in exact opposition to our Saviour's declaration, that he will reward every man *according to his works*: [83]and again, that it is "not the will of 'our' Father which is in heaven that one of those little ones," i.e. children, "should perish."[84] These declarations would, I think, sufficiently prove that St. Paul's expressions on the subject relate to national, and not individual election, even had the Apostle himself left his meaning unexplained: for the servant is not greater than his master, and it is not possible that an inspired Apostle should preach a doctrine different from that of Him who commissioned him; but if I mistake not, he has himself taken especial care that his meaning on this important subject should *not* be misunderstood. For first, it is a notorious fact, though often overlooked in argument, that the very passage, "I will have mercy on whom I will have mercy, and I will have compassion on whom I will have compassion," which is the main support claimed for the doctrine of absolute decrees, is quoted from Exodus, and forms the assurance given by God himself to Moses, that He had separated *the Hebrew nation* from all the people on the face of the earth. [85]Again St. Paul has asserted that God will render to *every* man *according to his deeds*, for there is

---

that it was not the wrath of God which required to be appeased by the great sacrifice—the slave was *bought by Him for Himself*—the price was of course paid to another. Much misunderstanding has arisen from the careless interpretation of these and the like passages, whose phraseology has become obsolete along with the practice of buying and selling slaves, at least in this country.

[83] Matt. xvi. 27.

[84] Matt. xviii. 14.

[85] Vide Exod. xxxiii. 14, et seq.

no respect of persons with God.[86] God will have *all men* to be saved, &c. &c.

God forbid that we should consider that a man may not be a sincere Christian, who believes himself irrevocably called, "elect," and inevitably secure of his salvation; or declare that a strict Calvinist cannot be attached to our church: but St. Paul teaches that "Christ died for all;" that grace instead of being irresistible may be received in vain; that those who have been once justified instead of being *sure* of "final perseverance" and salvation, *may* "sin wilfully after they have received the knowledge of the truth," and "draw back to perdition," so that it behoves every one "who thinketh he standeth to take heed lest he fall."[87]

In regard to "irresistible" (special) "grace," Scripture assures us that grace sufficient for salvation is denied to none; for St. Paul in every passage of the Epistles, which relates to grace, declares that the Spirit works in the souls of *all*, enabling them, if they do not obstinately resist it, "to work out their salvation." The following passage is taken from the work of a teacher of the doctrine of Special Grace. "The reign of sin consists not in the multitude, greatness or prevalency of sins, for all these are consistent with a state of grace, and may be in a child of God, in whom sin doth not and cannot reign; but in the in-being of sin without grace, whether it act more or less violently, yea, whether it acts at all or no: yet if the habit of sin possess the soul without any principle of grace implanted, which is contrary to it, that man may be said to be still under the dominion of sin. This mortification then of sin, as to its reigning power, is completed in

---

[86] According to the Calvinistic doctrine above stated, character has no concern whatever with their call; ergo, if this is right, St. Paul is wrong, and mankind *are* called with respect of persons.

[87] "This system (Calvinism) by setting aside the idea of a human will, leaves the doctrine of Divine Will barren and unmeaning; the idea of a personal ruler disappears, and those most anxious to assert the government of the Living God have been the great instruments in propagating the notion of an atheistical necessity." *Maurice's Kingdom of Christ.*

the first act of conversion and regeneration."[88] But this language is by no means that of St. Paul: for the writer makes grace the test of holiness; whereas the apostle, following therein the doctrine of his master,—"by their fruits ye shall know them,"—makes holiness the test of grace. Indeed the obscurity and perplexing nature of the doctrine above quoted, stands in no favourable contrast with the simple and clear declaration of the Saviour, that we "do not gather grapes of thorns, nor figs of thistles,"—and that therefore the heart must be known by the words and actions: and the no less decided and simple exposition of the doctrine of Christ, by the beloved disciple, "Little children, let no man deceive you: he that doeth righteousness is righteous . . . he that committeth sin is of the devil. Whosoever is born of God *doth not commit sin* . . . whosoever doeth not righteousness is not of God." [89]

The doctrine of the *total* depravity of human nature, it appears to me, cannot be proved from Scripture any more than the two former. St. John, whilst asserting that no man is wholly without sin, exhorts to efforts, and supposes a possible state of Christian perfection in his converts, wholly incompatible with a state of entire corruption: and St. Paul, though he clearly states that sin has brought all men under condemnation, and that the unspirituality of the flesh can only be successfully opposed by the influence of the Holy Spirit, does not declare the consequences of the Fall in terms such as we find in the Calvinistic writers—as "Man, instead of the image of God, was now become the image of the Devil; instead of the citizen of heaven, he was become the bond-slave of hell, having in himself no one part of his former purity, but being altogether spotted and defiled—now he seemed to be nothing else but a lump of sin." And again: "Man is of his own nature fleshly and corrupt, &c. without any spark of

---

[88] Hopkins on the New Birth.

[89] I John iii. 7–10, see also v. 21 of the same chapter, where our confidence towards God is shown to depend on the judgment of our own consciousness of wrong or well doing. The whole chapter is well worth the study of every Christian.

goodness in him; only given to evil thoughts and evil deeds."
Even human nature, if closely examined, does not bear testimony
to this as truth: for either the grace of God is accorded in such
large measure to man from his birth, that none can be considered
as wholly bad; or the utter corruption preached by Calvin does
not exist. All experience may be appealed to on this point, even
that of the persons who use the above language; for if they search
their own hearts in sincerity, they will become conscious of
amiable affections, and admiration of what is good and right:
neither, probably, are they guilty of any such gross and habitual
sins, as must mark a nature so wholly depraved. The Calvinist
therefore can only use these strong phrases with certain grains of
allowance: and he would be wiser if he were to avoid offending
his—if he prefer so to call him—weaker brother, by technical
terms which he himself cannot use in their *full force* before the
Searcher of hearts.

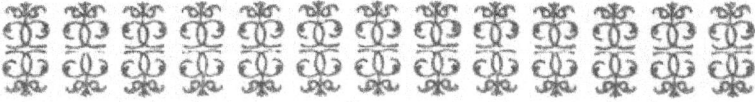

LETTER VII.

PRESBYTERIANS. INDEPENDENTS.

When the preaching of Luther and his coadjutors had effectually called men's attention to the affairs of the church, it was natural that questions with regard to its government no less than its doctrine, should be freely mooted. The usurpations of Rome had a tendency to disgust the Reformers with episcopal government, and accordingly we find both Calvin and Luther establishing a more republican form; and instead of giving the ecclesiastical power into the hands of one man, they judged it proper to delegate it to the elders (presbyters) of each church respectively; subject only to the control of the majority of a general synod. Such was the origin of what we now term Presbyterians as a sect: for in *England* more moderate councils, and the circumstance that the reformed tenets were embraced by many of the bishops, led to retaining the Episcopal form of church government. In *Scotland*, after a struggle, the Presbyterian form was finally established, and the church or kirk of that part of Great Britain is regulated upon that system. A secession has lately taken place on the question of the right of presentation to livings, but the *doctrine* taught in both is nearly similar, i.e. that of the Calvinistic churches.

The General Synod of Ulster (originally a branch of the established kirk of Scotland), is the principal body of Presbyterians considered as dissenters from the establishment: and there also, there is a Presbyterian Synod, or Church of "the Apostolic Seceders," formed by seceders from the General Synod, which is thoroughly Calvinistic, and which maintains the same discipline that is usually observed among the seceding "Scottish Presbyterians." In the reign of Geo. I. Arianism[90] was openly embraced by some of the more speculative of the Presbyterian ministers in Ireland, and in consequence, a theological controversy was carried on for twenty years (from 1705 to 1725), which ended in the secession of eight Arian ministers, and the formation of the Presbytery of Antrim. Some who were secretly inclined to Arianism had not the courage to follow the example of the eight seceders, and the leaven continued to spread among the general body during the latter part of the eighteenth century, till at length inquiries were instituted in the Synod, which led to a fresh separation. Seventeen at length seceded out of thirty-seven ministers, holding Arian or Socinian tenets in the year 1830, and they subsequently formed themselves into a distinct Synod, under the name of "the Remonstrant Synod of Ulster," and the Presbytery of Antrim has now become incorporated with this Synod. These Arian congregations are chiefly situated in the counties of Antrim and Down, in the north and eastern part of the province. There are ten or twelve congregations in the south of Ireland forming the Synod of Munster, which were also, till within a few years, Arian or Socinian. The total number of Remonstrant and Socinian congregations is between thirty and forty. *All* the Presbyterian bodies,—Orthodox and Arian, share in the Government grants known under the name of "Regium Donum." This royal bounty was originally dispensed among the Presbyterian clergy of Ulster in lieu of the tithes which were taken from them at the Restoration, and bestowed upon the Episcopal conformists. It was withdrawn towards the close of the reign of

---

[90] I take this from books, not having personal acquaintance with the Presbyterians of Ireland: and such is the confusion generally made by authors between Arianism, Socinianism, and Unitarianism, that it is difficult to know which is meant. As a large proportion of the modern Presbyterians have embraced Unitarian doctrines, it seems improbable that the Irish should have adopted those of Arius, though my author uses the term Arian as applied to the doctrine of the seceders.

Charles II.; but at the Revolution, letters patent passed the great seal of Ireland, granting £1200 per annum to seven Presbyterian ministers, during pleasure, for the use of the ministers of the north of Ireland, to be paid quarterly out of any of the revenues of the kingdom. This grant was renewed, under certain limitations, in the reign of Queen Anne: and in the reign of Geo. I. £800 per annum was divided in equal shares between the ministers of the Ulster Synod and those of the Southern Association. In 1784 an additional grant was made to the Ulster Synod of £1000 per annum. In 1792 the grant was augmented to £5000 to be divided among the ministers of the Synod,—the Presbytery of Antrim,—the Seceders,—the Southern Association,—and the ministers of the French church, Dublin. In 1803 some fresh regulations were made, by which the distribution of the bounty was taken immediately into the hands of Government, and the Presbyterian clergy were thus rendered more ostensibly what they had previously been only in effect, i.e., stipendiaries of the state. The congregations under the care of the several Synods and Presbyteries are now arranged in three classes according to the number of families and the stipend of each minister; and the allowance to the ministers of the three classes was fixed at £50, £75, and £100 per annum. The members of the congregation feel under no obligation to contribute much, if anything, to their pastor's support, who is therefore often compelled to have recourse to farming, grazing, or some other secular employment, for the support of his family.

"In 1834 the ascendant party in the Synod succeeded in carrying a resolution enforcing unqualified subscription to the "Confession of Faith," which had not previously been enforced. The ostensible motive for this is a desire to bring about a closer union with the Established Church of Scotland. The Irish Synod being now so far connected with the state as to form a species of ecclesiastical establishment, a feeling has been generated in favour of the established church of both countries: a strong protest, however has been made against the decision, but without avail." [91]

The increase of the Presbyterians in Ireland from whatever cause has borne no due proportion to that of the general population.

"Presbyterianism received as a scheme of policy, though admirably adapted to the exigencies of the times in which it originated, partakes of the essential defectiveness of the incipient reformation of the sixteenth century, embodying these erroneous principles which were adopted by the founders of most of the Protestant churches, and which soon proved not less fatal to the cause of scriptural truth than to the internal peace of the Christian communities."

The first Presbyterian church was founded in Geneva by John Calvin, about a.d. 1541, and the system afterwards introduced into Scotland, with modifications by John Knox, about the year 1560, but not *legally* established there till 1592. It has never flourished greatly in England, and the Unitarian doctrine has now been almost universally received among the quondam Presbyterian congregations.

The *theory* of discipline in the Scottish Church does not differ very widely from that of the English episcopacy, but the *practice* of the two churches, as modified by the habits of the two nations, is totally different. In order to reconcile the Anglican and Scottish confessions of faith, it would be requisite that the Church of England should consent to suppress Articles III. VII. XXXV. and XXXVI. also that part of Art. VI. which sanctions the public reading of the Apocrypha, and the first clause of Art. XX, attributing to the church a power to decree rites and ceremonies, as well as authority in controversies of faith. Agreeing, as the English and Scottish Churches do *substantially* in

---

[91] See "The Use and Abuse of Creeds and Confession of Faith," by the Rev. Charles James Carlile, Dublin, 1836. "The Irish Church and Ireland," p. 66–68, and "A Narrative of the Proceedings of the Associate Synod in Ireland and Scotland in the affair of the Royal Bounty," by James Bryce. Belfast, 1816.

the doctrines of the Protestant faith, they nevertheless differ widely,

1. As to the nature of holy orders and the power of ordination.

2. As to the hierarchical constitution of the Anglican Church.

3. As to matters of ritual, especially the use of liturgies which the Church of Scotland rejects.

4. As to the doctrines of sacramental grace and sacerdotal absolution, implied in the offices of the Anglican Church.

5. As to the whole system of discipline, Ecclesiastical Courts, &c.

6. As to certain points of Calvinistic theology.

The Independents differ from the Presbyterians chiefly in three points, namely:

1. As to ordination, and the liberty of preaching.

2. As to the political form and constitution of church government, and the conditions of church communion.

3. As to the grounds and limits of religious liberty.

"Ordination alone," say the Independents, "without the precedent consent of the Church by those who formerly have been advanced by virtue of that power they have received by their ordination, doth not constitute any person a church officer, or communicate office power unto him." The Presbyterians on the other hand deny that the mere invitation and choice of the people could confer the pastoral office, or that it was even a prerequisite. The Independents seem to have identified the ministerial function with the pastoral office; and argued that it was absurd to ordain an officer without a province to exercise the office in. Their opponents viewed the Christian ministry more as an order invested with certain inherent powers; a faculty or profession endowed with peculiar privileges, the admission into which required to be jealously guarded; and this power and authority they conceive could be transmitted by those of the order. All approved candidates for the ministerial office among the Presbyterians, are ordained without reference to any local change; among the Independents no probationer is ordained till he has been appointed to the pastoral office. The first Independent or Congregational Church in England was established by a Mr. Jacob, a.d. 1616, though it is asserted that a Mr. Robinson was the founder of this sect, of which Dr. John Owen, Dr. Isaac Watts, Dr. Doddridge, and Job Orton were members.

The following extracts are from the discourses of Robert Hall, who, though a Baptist, dissented from most of his brethren on the subject of strict communion. He was a preacher both of Baptist and Independent congregations, but he did not hesitate to avow that "he had more fellowship of feeling for an Independent or a Presbyterian than for a close communion Baptist." His system of theological tenets was on the model of what has come to be denominated "Moderate Calvinism." With regard to the distinctive Calvinistic doctrine of Predestination, "I cannot," says his biographer, "answer for the precise terms in which he would have stated it, but I presume he would have accepted those employed by the Church of England. In preaching he very rarely made any express reference to that doctrine."

"Jesus Christ did not come, let it be remembered, to establish a mere external morality, that his followers might be screened from human laws and human justice, for human laws will take care of this. The holy institution of Christianity has a nobler object, that of purifying our hearts and regulating our behaviour by the love of God. In the most practical accounts of the proceedings of the last day given in the Scriptures, the excellency which is represented as being a criterion and distinguishing feature of the disciple of Christ, and which He will acknowledge, is: Christian benevolence—love to man manifested in the relief of the poor. The Apostle St. John has given us a most sublime description of the love of God, when he says, 'God is love;' love is not so much an attribute of His nature as His *very essence*, the spirit of Himself. Christian benevolence is not only the 'image of God,' but is peculiarly an imitation of Christ." "I do not ask, my brethren, what particular virtue you have, but *how much are you under the influence of Him?* for just so much virtue we have, as we have of His spirit and character." "Our Saviour places the acceptance of men, not upon their dispositions, but upon their actions; upon what *they have done,* not upon what they have *merely believed* or *felt,* or in any undefined state of mind."—"I am persuaded that the cause of the ruin of professing Christians does not arise so much from a mistake of the doctrines of Christianity as from a low idea of Christian morals; in abstaining from certain crimes and disorders through fear of the loss of character and of punishment, without reflecting on the spirit of that holy religion which we profess."—"Christ went about doing good, not as an *occasional* exercise, but as his *employment;* it was the one thing which he did. Though possessed of infinite power, he never employed it in resenting or retaliating an injury. He was pre-eminently devout. His was an active life; it was not the life of a solitary monk. That devotion which terminates in itself is a luxury which sometimes perverts the principles of benevolence to a pernicious purpose. Let us rather recede from being called Christians than forget the great symbol of our profession, love to one another."

LETTER VIII.

PARTICULAR BAPTISTS, SUB AND SUPRALAPSARIANS, SANDEMANIANS.

Having now given some account of the principal Calvinistic sects, I shall conclude by mentioning a few of those less numerous societies, which, whilst agreeing in the peculiar doctrines of Calvin, differ upon other points. The particular baptists, agreeing with the General Baptists on most other practices and doctrines, differ from them on this. The separation took place in the year 1616, when a controversy on the subject of infant baptism having arisen among the Baptists, one portion calling itself the "Independent Congregation" seceded, embraced the Calvinistic doctrine, and became the first Particular Baptists: others, who were in general attached to the opinions of Calvin, concerning the decrees of God and Divine Grace, were not entirely agreed concerning the manner of explaining the doctrine of the Divine decrees. The greater part believed that God only *permitted* the first man to fall into transgression, without particularly predetermining his fall: these were termed sublapsarians. But others again maintained that "God in order to exercise and display his justice and his free mercy, had decreed from all eternity the transgression of Adam, and so ordered the course of events, that our first parents could not possibly avoid their fall. These were termed supralapsarians.

There is a modern sect that originated in Scotland about 1728, termed Glassites, from its founder Mr. John Glass, who was expelled by the Synod from the Church of Scotland, for maintaining that "the kingdom of Christ was not of this world." His adherents then formed themselves into churches, conformable in their institution and discipline to what they apprehended to be the plan of the first churches recorded in the New Testament. Soon after the year 1755, Mr. John Sandeman (an elder in one of these congregations in Scotland) attempted to prove that "Faith is neither more nor less than a simple assent to the Divine testimony, concerning Jesus Christ delivered for the offences of men and raised again for their justification, as recorded in the New Testament." He also mentioned that the word *Faith* or *Belief*, is constantly used by the Apostles to signify what is denoted by it in common conversation, i.e. a persuasion of the truth of any proposition, and that there is no difference between believing any common testimony, and believing the apostolic testimony, except that which results from the testimony itself, and the Divine authority on which it rests. This led to controversy among the Calvinists and Sandemanians, concerning the nature of justifying faith; and the latter formed themselves into a separate sect. They administer the sacrament of the Lord's supper weekly, and hold "love feasts," of which every member is not only allowed but required to partake, and which consists of their dining together at each other's houses, in the interval between the morning and afternoon service. They interpret literally the precept respecting the "kiss of charity," which they use on the admission of a new member, as well as on other occasions, when they deem it necessary or proper: they make a weekly collection before the sacrament of the Lord's supper; use mutual exhortation; abstain from blood and things strangled; wash each other's feet; hold that every one is to consider all that he possesses to be liable to the calls of the poor and the church, and that it is unlawful to "lay up treasure upon earth," by setting them apart for any future use. They allow of public and private diversions, so far as they are not connected with circumstances really sinful;

but apprehending a lot to be sacred, they disapprove of lotteries, playing at cards, dice, &c. They maintain the necessity of a plurality of elders, pastors, or bishops in each church, and the necessity of the presence of two elders in every act of discipline, and at the administration of the Lord's supper. Second marriages disqualify for the office of elder. The elders are ordained by prayer and fasting, imposition of hands, and giving the "right hand of fellowship." In their discipline they are strict and severe, and in every transaction esteem unanimity to be absolutely necessary.

LETTER IX.
CALVINISTIC METHODISTS.
EVANGELICAL OR SERIOUS
CHRISTIANS.

I noticed the name of George Whitfield when speaking of Wesley and his followers, for during a time they acted in unison; Whitfield, however, soon embraced the Calvinistic tenets, and then the friends separated with much of unkindly feeling. Wesley held the doctrines of Calvin in abhorrence, as altogether unchristian and unfounded in Scripture. "I defy you to say so hard a thing of the Devil," said he with characteristic earnestness, when speaking of the notion that God could arbitrarily create any for eternal reprobation. This separation between the leaders soon extended to their congregations, and from that time Calvinistic and Wesleyan Methodists became distinct sects, differing, however, but little on any other point, excepting in the greater tendency to enthusiasm among the followers of Whitfield.

"Wesley and Whitfield," says Mr. Sidney in his life of Rowland Hill, "were men of widely different characters, both in respect to their natural dispositions as well as the discipline of their minds; and painful frailties were visible in the midst of their true greatness. An ambitious love of power was evidently the besetting weakness of John Wesley; aspiration to the *honours* when he had no prospect of the *suffering* of martyrdom, was that of Whitfield." In his letters to Rowland Hill, it is evident how he courted and enjoyed persecution; and whenever "*the fire* (to use his own expression) was kindled in the country;" he was not satisfied unless "honoured" by being scorched a little in its flame. This was a wrong spirit, and did injury to his own mind, and to his followers, by encouraging a morose and morbid carriage towards the world, giving needless offence, and provoking animosity in those who might have been attracted and endeared to truth by the lovely graces of pure Christianity."

At the time when he, and his early friends the Wesleys began their ministry, the piety of all classes was at a very low ebb. The earnestness of these men gave a new impulse to religious feeling, and after a time a considerable number of other episcopally ordained ministers of the church, together with a portion of the laity, became influenced by the same sentiments. Without seceding, they formed a party in the church, leaning to Calvinism to the extent they thought justified by the xxxix Articles; and this party soon became designated by several distinguishing terms. They called themselves *Evangelical* first, afterwards when that became a cant term of misapplied reproach, they took the title of *Serious* Christians, and by others were called *Low Church*, and *Methodistical.* Besides distinguishing themselves by an especial name, they avoided public amusements, used a peculiar phraseology, and seemed to delight in wearing their religion externally in the sight of all men, thinking perhaps to reform the thoughtless by the example of their greater strictness. But herein, in my opinion, they made a net for their own feet, for that very aspiration after greater exaltation which is implanted in us as a spur to strive after glory and immortality, is soon by mismanagement perverted into a love of earthly distinction. Hence comes ambition; but the ambition for worldly honours has in it this alleviation, that the man who toils after a title or a fortune, knows that he is, after all, seeking but a mean object; and if ever his mind is awakened at all to a sense of the world to come, the soul springs back to its true ambition, and launches into the career natural to it: but the man who seeks to be distinguished among his brethren for superior holiness, and wears it externally, that it may be seen and honoured by men, blinds his better nature, and fetters it to earth by chains forged in heaven; he sees not that he is ambitious; he is not aware that while seeking, as he imagines, to honour God in his life, he is enjoying at his heart's core the respectful homage of men; and whilst attending to his outward deportment, and making a display even of his humility, he too frequently leaves the inner heart unchastened. Our Saviour knew the frailties of man, and his injunction that our religion should chiefly be manifested by our benevolent feelings towards our fellow creatures, while the communing with God should be carried on in silence and secrecy, is the only safe guide in these matters.

I have no doubt that there are many of the Low Church party, whose conscientiousness sets at defiance the dangers of the system they have adopted: indeed my own private friendships warrant me in saying so: but it is not well to lead others into dangerous paths where our own skill indeed may enable us to walk safely, but where the hindmost, whom we are not leading by the hand, are in continual hazard of deviating from the true course; and therefore whilst honouring individual virtues, I continue to consider the whole system erroneous: one whose tendency is to create spiritual pride, and lower the standard of Christian benevolence by restricting to a party that fellowship which should be universal. It does but substitute the excitement of the crowded church where a popular preacher charms with all the graces of rhetoric, of the committee room, of the speakers at Exeter Hall, for the ball room and the theatre; with this difference, that in the first case the instinct which makes the mind seek this excitement, is overlooked; the man believes himself performing a meritorious action, and looks with some contempt on his weaker brethren, who cannot exist without worldly amusements; on the other he knows what he is about, and if he be well-intentioned, guards against excess. It would be wiser therefore to acknowledge the instinct; not bad in itself, for God implanted it, and if it be denied a due indulgence, the mind sinks into hopeless imbecility; and not to blame those who seek other, but innocent means of gratifying it.[92]

The extracts that I am about to give, from the writings of two men of note, in that party, distinguished also for their genuine Christian feeling, will show that they saw the dangers I have pointed out, and were anxious to guard against them. The following extracts are given in Mr. Sidney's "Life of the Rev. Rowland Hill." [93]

"I hate dry doctrinal preaching, without warm, affectionate, and experimental applications. Oh! 'tis most pleasant to love one another with pure hearts fervently. Love is of God, for 'God is love.' The summit of our happiness must be the perfection of our holiness. By this blessed grace we have the brightest evidence that we are 'born of God.' If we allow that little shades of difference may exist, we ought to 'love as brethren,' and where Christian

---

[92] Although the excellent Bishop Heber's mind was deeply imbued with devotional feelings, he considered a moderate participation in what are usually called worldly amusements, to be allowable and blameless. "He thought," says his biographer, "that the strictness which made no distinction between things blameable only in their abuse, and the practices which were really immoral, was prejudicial to the interests of true religion; and on this point his opinion remained unchanged to the last. His own life indeed was a proof that amusement so participated in, may be perfectly harmless, and no way interfere with any religious or moral duty."

[93] "Rowland Hill, in his theological opinions, leaned towards Calvinism, but what is called Hyper-calvinism, he could not endure. In a system of doctrine he was follower of no man, but drew his sermons fresh from a prayerful reading of the Bible. He was for drawing together all the people of God wherever they could meet, and was willing to join in a universal communion with Christians of every name. When, on one occasion, he had preached in a chapel, where none but baptized adults (i.e. baptized after attaining years of discretion), were admitted to the sacrament, he wished to have communicated with them, but was told respectfully, 'You cannot sit down at *our* table.' He calmly replied, 'I thought it was the Lord's table.'" Sidney's Life of R. Hill, p. 422, 3rd Edit.

candour and love are found to reign, the odious sin of schism, according to its general interpretation, cannot exist." "It is no sign that we value the blessings of God, if we can part with them" (i.e. dear friends) "without regret. That mind is badly framed that prefers stoical indifference to Christian sensibility, and though the pain is abundantly more acute where those finer feelings of the mind are found to exist; yet who deserves the name of a human being who is without them?" "While a soul within our reach is ignorant of a Saviour, we must endeavour to win it to Christ. How weary I am of a great deal of what is called the 'religious world!' High and Low Church Sectarianism seems to be the order of the day; we are much more busy in contending for *parties* than for *principles*. These evils are evidences of a lack of genuine Christianity. Oh! when shall that happy day dawn upon us, when real Christians and Christian ministers of all denominations shall come nearer to each other."

The next extracts shall be from the writings of one who was scarcely appreciated by the world in general, but of whose excellencies I was enabled to judge, during my residence at Cambridge; Mr. Simeon.

"Religion appears in its true colours when it regulates our conduct in social life; your religion must be seen, not in the church, or in the closet only, but in the shop, the family, the field: it must mortify pride and every other evil passion, and must bring faith into exercise. Try yourselves by this standard: see what you are as husbands or wives, parents or children, masters or servants[94]."

"The self-righteous, self-applauding moralist can spy out the failings and infirmities of those who profess a stricter system of religion; but let me ask such an one, 'Are there not in thee, even in thee, sins against the Lord thy God?' Verily if thou wouldst consult thy own conscience, thou wouldst see little reason, and feel little inclination too, to cast stones at others. Professors of religion also are but too guilty of this same fault,

---

[94] Simeon's Works, Vol. III. p. 101, &c.

being filled with an overweening conceit of their own excellencies, and a contemptuous disregard of their less spiritual neighbours. But I would ask the professed follower of Christ, Are there not sins with thee too as well as with the pharisaic formalist? Are there not great and crying evils in the religious world, which prove a stumbling block to those around them? Are there not often found among professors of religion the same covetous desires, the same fraudulent practices, the same deviations from truth and honour, as are found in persons who make no profession? Are there not many whose tempers are so unsubdued, that they make their whole families a scene of contention and misery? Yes! Though the accusations which are brought against the whole body of religious people as 'hypocrites,' are a gross calumny, there is but too much ground for them in the conduct of many." "Nothing is more common, and nothing more delusive than a noisy, talkative religion. True religion is a humble, silent, retired thing; not affecting public notice, but rather wishing to approve itself to God. It is not in *saying* 'Lord, Lord!' but in *doing* the will of our heavenly Father, that we shall find acceptance at the last day. Happy would it be if many who place all their religion in running about and hearing sermons, and talking of the qualifications of ministers, would attend to this hint, and endeavour to acquire more of that wisdom which evinces its Divine origin by the excellence of its fruits." [95]

---

[95] Simeon's Works, Vol. III. p. 333.

LETTER X.

ON ROMANISM AND CEREMONIAL RELIGION.

I promised that as the completion of my task, I would notice those differences which have occurred in the bosom of the church itself, even though they can scarcely be called *sects*; I therefore propose to conclude my correspondence with a short survey of the above-named, which I think should rather be viewed as the working out of great principles, than as parties distinguished by particular creeds or opinions on abstract subjects. I may run counter to some prejudices, perhaps, in so doing; but the truth is well worth running a tilt for:—you may sit by as umpire, and decide when I have done, whether I have carried my spear in a knightly fashion.

Though I shall not think it necessary, like Racine's advocate in Les Plaideurs, to go back to the Assyrians and the Babylonians to illustrate my proposition, yet I must begin from a very distant period, in order to make my views thoroughly comprehensible. I must therefore beg you to notice that the tendency of man's mind always is, and always has been, towards the visible and the tangible. The pure abstraction of a Governing Will without any perceptible presence, has in it something too remote from the common habits, powers, and feelings of human nature, ever to be thoroughly embraced by the heart of man; and we find that the Deity has always condescended so far to the weakness of his creatures, as to give the imagination some resting place. Thus the patriarch had his altar of sacrifice, where the fire from heaven marked the present Deity—and the Israelite had first the pillar of the cloud, and then the tabernacle, where the mysterious Shechinah dwelt over the mercy seat. Yet even this indistinct representation of an embodied Deity, did not satisfy the people: they required a *form*, tangible, visible, and Aaron yielded to the wish; because he thought it a prudent and allowable compliance with the weakness of human nature. He was wrong, and was punished for it; and this transaction we shall find the type and foreshadowing of every thing that has since happened in the world with regard to religion. The Almighty gives man just enough to rest his thoughts upon: it is the fire on the altar, the cloud, the temple, and last of all *the man*, in whom our devotion may find also an object of affection: but he requires that we shall not go beyond this. We must not return to earth, and make for ourselves a worship less spiritual than he has instituted; on the contrary, he requires us to pierce through the veil as we advance in knowledge, and discern the spiritual through the visible. Hence the perpetual denunciations of the prophets against the Jews for their adherence to forms, which latterly they did adhere to, instead of giving attention to the purification of their hearts.

Among all but the Israelites, the progress of the tangible was much more rapid: idolatry, with all its gross rites, had established itself among *the people*, at any rate, in Egypt, at a very early period; and spread from that old and luxurious empire, through the more simple states which sprang up around and from it. The Exodus was a warning from on high, that there was a Being, unseen and intangible, whose fiat governed all things: and this lesson was not wholly without fruit: yet still the human race reverted to the objects of the senses, till, in God's good time, he sent his Son: presented a tangible form on which the mind could dwell—then removed it from the earth, and said, "You may now think on this, and give your imagination a resting place: this form you shall see again; but in mean time you must purify your hearts from earthly desires: that form will only greet your eyes when you have cast off the burthen of the flesh, and have entered upon a spiritual existence." The first Christians remembered and loved the man; his precepts, his example, his smallest words or actions were recurred to with the fondness of personal friendship; and this carried Christianity through the first two centuries; but then this remembrance began to have a character of abstraction, and again the human heart called for tangibility. Then came, step by step, gorgeous ceremonies, pictures, representations of the personal presence and sufferings of the Saviour. The very requirements of those who quitted the splendid and sensual rites of heathenism for the faith of Christ, led the Christian doctors to endeavour to replace the festival of the idol by something analogous in the Christian church: and thus without well knowing what they were tending to, the heads of the church yielded one point of spiritualism after another; sought to captivate and awe the people by impressive ceremonies; and finished by the sin of Aaron: they set up the image and said, "These be thy Gods, O Israel! that brought thee out of the land of Egypt."[96] For be it observed here, that Aaron set up this image merely as a tangible representation of the true Deity; *a help to the devotion of the people*, who could not worship without seeing something.

This then is Romanism; it is not transubstantiation, nor the mediation of the Virgin and the Saints,[97] nor the infallibility of popes and councils; these are natural consequences indeed, but the distinctive character of the Romish church is *tangibility*. "There is the actual flesh," it says, "there is the representation of the actual human presence of saints and martyrs; there is the actual man enthroned, who represents the power of God:" but it might have fifty other ways of satisfying this restless craving of the human mind, and it would be equally pernicious in any of these forms. Man's great struggle has always been between the animal and the spiritual nature, and when religion goes one step farther towards tangibility than the Deity himself has allowed, the animal nature gains strength; and vice and licentiousness follow as naturally, among the mass of the people, as rain follows the cloud.

---

[96] Exod. xxxii. 4.
[97] Vide Colossians ii. 18, 19.

Observe, I do not here deny that many may profess a religion of sense, and remain spiritually-minded themselves: Heathenism had its Socrates, its Xenocrates, &c.—Romanism has its Pascal, its Fenelon, and a train of other great names: but look at the *people* during that period, and the account will be very different. When an ignorant man imagines that he can remove the Divine anger by a sacrifice or a penance, he avoids the trouble of curbing his passions, and compounds, as he thinks, for indulgence of the one, by the performance of the other; but when he is told that purity of life and thought is the only road to Divine favour, if he sins, he sins at least with some feelings of compunction, some dread that he may not have it in his power to remove the stain he is incurring. The preaching of Wesley reformed multitudes, all enthusiastic as it was; but it would be difficult to find a parallel in the annals of Romanism. As great a movement of the public mind was made by the preaching of Peter the Hermit; but how different was the object and the result! The personal pilgrimage to the Holy Sepulchre, as a mode of wiping out sin, was undertaken by thousands, who perished miserably, or, if they lived, came back not better men than they went: under a system of less tangibility, and a preaching as effective, they might have staid in their homes, and glorified God by a life such as Christ came to teach and to exemplify.

It is so much easier to make a pilgrimage, or endure a long fast, than to subdue and tame the animal nature till it becomes obedient to the rational will, and seconds instead of resisting its wishes, that it is not surprising that in all ages a religion of outward observance should be more popular than one of inward purification. Those even which set off with the highest pretensions in this way have degenerated, and the outward and visible form is too often substituted for the inward and spiritual grace, which it was intended to *represent* not to *supersede*. That religion therefore has the best chance of influencing the soul, which, as far as is possible, renounces outward demonstrations which human indolence is so glad to rely on, and preaches boldly and effectually the uselessness of ceremonies, farther than as they tend to preserve the remembrance of Him who came to call the world back to Himself, to trample on the sensual and the animal, and to raise man to his pristine, or rather, to what is to be his future state. A public acknowledgment of Christ as our Master and Lord, and a compliance with his own few and simple ordinances; are all that Christian duty requires, and nearly as much as Christian prudence will permit. The rest is a matter of worldly expediency, and should be so regarded.

No doubt rests on my own mind—I leave others to think as they may—that Episcopacy was the established form of the Church as soon as the Christian communities began to assume enough of regularity to admit of any settled order; and I think it a wise form. As far as any institution can, it secures unity and decency in the church: and as far as any institution can, that was not positively established by Christ himself, it possesses, in my mind, the sanction of antiquity. It gives the concentration of purpose and regularity of effort which is bestowed by the discipline of an army; for as in an army a detachment acts upon the same system of tactics, and obeys officers constituted by the same authority, and thus assists the efforts of the main body, and falls into rank with it when they meet; so the church, under such a form, may send detachments to the ends of the earth, who may meet after long years, as brothers of the same communion, and find that though the individuals have passed away, others have stepped into their place in the ranks, and are teaching what their predecessors taught. The benefit of church discipline, therefore, in my mind is great; but I do not suppose that salvation depends on it, because God has repeatedly declared that Christ died *for all*,[98] and that he is not willing that any should perish;[99] consequently he can hardly have made our eternal state dependent on what no man can accomplish for himself. A person may not have it in his power to receive baptism from an ordained priest, but he may live as Christ taught; or, having never heard of Christ

---

[98] 2 Cor. v. 15. I Tim. ii. 6.
[99] 2 Pet. iii. 9.

even, he may, like the gentiles, win glory and immortality,[100] if, having not the law, he be a law unto himself. I would not receive Christ's ordinances from the hands of any but an ordained priest, myself, because if a doubt exist in my mind, I sin in doing the doubtful thing; but herein I speak only for myself; let every man do as he is "persuaded in his mind" [101]in matters of secondary import, as all ceremonial matters must be.

You will now be prepared for my opinion with regard to the late movement made in the church by the Anglo-Catholics, as they term themselves; Puseyites, or Newmanites, as they have been termed by others. They have been thought to have introduced innovations—they have not:—there is not one of the ceremonies or practices which they have recommended, which was not very early practised in the church; but it was from the undue importance attached to these ceremonies, which came to be regarded with reverence from having been instituted by apostles and martyrs, that the after growth of Roman superstition sprang up so rankly. I believe the first promoters of this movement were as remote from actual Romanism as I am, when they first began it; but when once reason is submitted to any human dictum, in matters of religion, there is no resting place till we arrive at the "infallible" guide which the Romish church claims to be. There alone can the soul which will not think for itself, find a ready and confident director. Accordingly, we find that some of those very men who but a few years back exposed the errors of Romanism, have now yielded themselves blindfold to the guidance of that very church, which, as long as they allowed themselves to reason, they acknowledged to have departed from the truth. Yet it is perhaps fortunate for the people generally, that this declension of its pastors has been as rapid and complete as it has been:—they were going back towards the sin of Aaron—they were insisting on ceremonies as necessary to salvation, thus rendering religion gross and tangible, and the people thus taught would soon have forgotten what those ceremonies were intended to represent, and

---

[100] Rom. ii. 6–11.
[101] Rom. xiv. 5.

have depended for salvation on what could not avail them in the hour of need: for the repetition of prayer is not necessarily praying, nor is the reception of the eucharist necessarily sanctification, though these may be the outward and visible signs of the inward and spiritual grace which is working in the heart. Once teach a man that *any* ceremony is *requisite* to salvation, and he will soon go a step further by himself, and think the outward ceremony sufficient without the inward grace. This indeed is but a necessary corollary; for if the ceremony be requisite to salvation, then the inward grace working purity of life, avails not without the ceremony; and thus purity of life is no longer a substantive virtue; it cannot stand alone; and the prop which it requires being so very strong, why should not the prop itself be all in all? This will be the course of ratiocination in the mind of the mass of mankind, whether avowed or not; and however the promoters of a ceremonial religion may shrink from such a consequence, it is so certain, as all experience shows, that they might as well throw a man who cannot swim into the water, and recommend him not to drown, as give a half instructed man a ceremony, which he is told is requisite to salvation, and expect that he will not cling to that, as the more convenient and least difficult observance; and whilst perfect in complying with every ordinance of the church, forget that he has overlooked the weightier matters of the law— judgment, justice, and mercy.

This may sound harsh, but it is true; and I appeal to the calm judgment even of the excellent Dr. Pusey himself, who has so unintentionally drawn many into a course from which, haply, he would now gladly draw them back, whether it be not so? His learning will show him how, through all ages, the spiritualism taught from heaven, has been counteracted by the visible and the tangible contrived by man; and in the step from the patriarchal religion, to the idolatry of Greece and Rome; from Christianity as preached by Christ and his Apostles, to the gross superstitions of the twelfth, thirteenth, and fourteenth centuries, he may see a type of what would be the consequence of again enforcing a ceremonial religion.

APPENDIX.

The following are extracts from the "Christianæ Religionis Institutio," of Faustus Socinus:

Q. Quid igitur de Dei natura, sive essentia, nosse omnino nos debere statuis?

R. Hæc duo in summa. Quod sit et quod unus tantum sit.

* * * * *

Q. Verum quid quæso saltem de Spiritu Sancto nunc mihi dicis de quo isti similiter affirmant eum esse divinam personam, nempe tertiam, et unum atque eundem numero Deum cum Patre et Filio?

R. Nempe illum non esse personam aliquam a Deo cujus est spiritus, distinctam, sed tantum modo (ut nomen ipsum *Spiritus,* quod flatum et afflationem, ut sic loquar, significat, docere potest) ipsius Dei vim et efficaciam quandam, id est eam, quæ secum sanctitatem aliquam afferat.

* * * * *

Q. Quid censes de Christi natura sive essentia nobis cognitii esse necessarium?

R. Id, ut antea dixi, sine cujus cognitione voluntas Dei erga nos per ipsum Christum patefacta, a nobis vel sciri, vel servari nequeat.

Q. Quid igitur ex iis quæ ad Christi naturam sive essentiam pertinent, ejusmodi esse censes?

R. Vix quidquam. Nam quædam, quæ ad ipsius Christi personam alioqui pertinent, et nobis omnino ob prædictam causam cognita esse debent, non naturalia illi sunt, sed a Deo postmodum ipsi data et concessa, et sic ad Dei voluntatem sunt referenda, et quidem ad primam quam fecimus ejus partem, id est ad Dei operationes.

Q. Quæ nam sunt ista?

R. Divinum imperium quod in nos habet. Rom. xiv. 9.; et suprema illa majestas. Ephes. i. 20, &c.; qua quidquid usquam est, aut excogitari potest, præter unam tantum ipsius Dei majestatem longe excellit. I Cor. xv. 27. Phil. ii. 8, 9. Heb. ii. 9. Hæc enim Christo haud naturalia esse, sed a Deo Patre illi data fuisse, ipsumque ea per et propter mortem atque obedientiam et resurrectionem suam adeptum esse, apertissime scriptura testatur.

Q. Cur vero hæc de Christo cognoscere omnino debemus?

R. Quia, ut Christum divino cultu officiamus vult Deus. Joh. v. 25. Psal. xlv. 12. Heb. i. 6. Philip. ii. 10.; ejus generis, inquam, cultu cujus is est, quem ipsi Deo exhibere debemus.

✻ ✻ ✻ ✻

Q. Quid de ipsa tamen Christi essentia seu natura statuis?

R. De Christi essentia ita statuo, illum esse hominem. Rom. v. 15.; in virginis utero, et sic sine viri ope, divini spiritus vi conceptum ac formatum. Matt. i. 20. 23. Luc. i. 35.; indeque genitum, primum quidem patibilem ac mortalem. 2 Cor. xiii. 4.; donec, scilicet munus sibi a Deo demandatum hie in terris obivit; deinde vero postquam in cœlum ascendit, impatibilem et immortalem factum. Rom. vi. 9.

✻ ✻ ✻ ✻

Q. Quid enim primum sibi vult, quod innuis hoc quod Christus Dei filius sit proprius et unigenitus non omnino ad ejus naturam pertinere?

R. Divina ista Christi filiatio, eatenus tantum ad ejus naturam aliquo modo referri potest, quatenus id respicit quod Christus divini Spiritus vi sine viri ope in virginis utero conceptus et formatus fuit. Nam hujusce rei causa eum Dei filium vocatum ire, ipsius Dei Angelus ipsimet virgini, ex qua natus est, prædixit. Luc. i. 35; et quidem consequenter Dei filium proprium et unigenitum, cum nemo alius hac ratione, et ab ipso primo ortu Dei films unquam extiterit.

✻ ✻ ✻ ✻

R. Quod attinet ad primum testimonium quod habetur (i.e. of præexistence) Joh. i. 3. Dictio universalis *omnia* non prorsus universaliter accipienda est, sed ad subjectam materiam restringenda, ut scilicet ea tantum omnia complectatur, quæ ad Evangelium pertinent.

Q. Sed quid dices, quod in loco isto apud Johannem additur; sine verbo, id est Deo filio, nihil esse factum?

R. Immo cum certum esse videatur, mox sequentia verba *quod factum est* (quidquid nonnulli contra sentiant) cum additione ista conjungenda esse: dicendum potius videtur, voluisse Evangelistam cum ista addidit indicare se de quibusdam nunquam antea et nova ac mirabili ratione factis loqui. Nam ad docendum simpliciter se loqui de iis quæ sunt facta nec semper fuerunt, satis habebat illa verba addere, *et sine ipso factum est nihil.* Itaque mysterio non videtur carere, quod præterea addit *quod factum est;* subaudi novum et mirabile, ad mundi ipsius statum pertinens, &c. &c.

✳ ✳ ✳ ✳ ✳

Jam dictum est (est de pœnis persolvendis primum agamus) pœnam quam uniusquisque nostrum propter delicta sua pendere tenebatur, mortem æternam esse. Hanc profecto Christus non subiit; et si cam subiisset, universi salutis nostræ et liberationis a peccatorum pœna spes, et ratio funditus eversa fuisset. Immo si jam Christus non resurrexisset, vana, ut inquit Paulus. I Cor. xv. 14, 17.; esset Evangelii prædicatio, et nos adhuc essemus in peccatis nostris. Et tamen, si idcirco nos servasset Christus, quod pœnas nostris peccatis debitas ipse sustinuisset, et nobis ejus rei fides quoad ejus fieri poterat facienda fuisset; eum nunquam resurgere, sed in morte perpetuo manere oportuisset: Op. Vol. p. 197, fol. Edit.

Ac dicitis, ut conjeci potest, animadvertendum esse, aliam in ipsa essentia divina personam patris esse, aliam personam filii: et Patri potuisse a Filio satisfieri seu ut satisfierat, vim suppeditari: nec tamen aliquid quod satisfactioni per solutionem facienda adversetur, committi. Sed dicite obsecro, nonne ipsius filii personæ non minus quam patris satisfaciendum fuisse affirmatis. Si filius patri satisfacit, hoc est, quod illi debetur solvit: quis ipsi filio, quod ipsi debetur, dabit? Respondebitis, ut arbitror, si patri satisfactum fuit, filio quoque satisfactum esse; cum eadem sit utriusque voluntas . . . Quomodo patri a filio quidquam ullo parto solvi potuisset si quod unius aut est, aut fit, alterius reipsa esse necesse foret? . . . At vero quis deinde ambigere queat filium patri nihil dare posse: cum quidquid filius habet patris revera sit, et ipse Christus disertè dixerit, Joh. xvii. 10, omnia quæ sua erant patris esse? Annon ex ipsa disciplina vestra, hoc est Dei essentiam non distinguere, sed partiri: si præter personarum proprietates, aliquid unam personam habere velitis quod alia non habeat. Filii autem personam proprietates suas patris personæ pro peccatorum nostrorum satisfactione solvisse, cui unquam in mentem venire poteret? Ib. p. 202.

FINIS.

www.ingramcontent.com/pod-product-compliance
Lightning Source LLC
Chambersburg PA
CBHW071744090426
42738CB00011B/2562